PUBLIC SPENDING FOR PUBLIC BENEFIT

How the public sector can use its purchasing power to deliver local economic development

Public spending for public benefit is a report, a lobbying tool, a new source of evidence, and a recommendation for future action based on what some people are doing already. We will cut to the heart of the matter: money. And show you why you can't afford not to care about how the public sector delivers goods and services.

Contents

Executive summary 1

Part 1: Talking the talk 3

Introduction 4

Ground rules 8

Defining jargon 10

Public spending for public benefit 13

Valuing the local economy 25

Lessons for the future 35

Recommendations 43

Part 2: Walking the walk 47

Case studies overview 48

Food 50

Construction 65

Waste minimisation 74

Youth services 84

Back office services 91

Resources 102

Acknowledgements 104

What will I gain from this report?

I am...	What will I gain?
In the public sector	**Ways to deliver better services for less money!**
Procurement	The evidence you need to convince your colleagues to re-think the role of procurement in promoting regeneration and to forge links between departments
Regeneration	The evidence you need to get your purchasing/procurement department to rethink their role in promoting regeneration
Finance	The evidence you need to show other departments why they should approach service delivery in a different way
Elsewhere	The evidence you need to show that promoting regeneration can be an integrated part of all public spending
In the private sector	**Persuasive evidence to open up doors at the public bodies in your area!**
Small business	Get your local public bodies to change their practices to open the playing field to small businesses like you
Large business	Get public bodies to see why they should take a proactive role in developing supply chains that help you deliver cheaper services
Social enterprise	Get public bodies to recognise the value you provide to the community and why they should work with you to deliver public services
In the community	**Persuasive evidence to get the public bodies in your area to listen!**
Community organisation	Get the public bodies in your area to engage with you first in finding ways to deliver public services
Support organisation	Get the public bodies in your area to think about how you can help them deliver public services by working with local suppliers and labour
Concerned resident	Get the public bodies in your area to take you seriously

Executive summary

The case (page 4)

- The UK public sector spends £125 billion per year on delivering goods and services.

- If the UK public sector steered just 10 per cent more of everyday spending on goods and services into the country's most disadvantaged areas, this would amount to £12.5 billion of income injected into those areas, *in just one year*.

- This £12.5 billion amounts to more than *17 times* the UK's annual spending on regeneration, which is £725 million.

- UK public bodies – including local authorities, hospitals, and schools – can deliver both regeneration and savings targets by developing solutions to local problems that promote local economic linkages.

- Solutions exist across a spectrum of public goods and services, including traditional 'back office' services, like premises cleaning.

The evidence (page 48)

- Cornwall Food Programme generates £47,000 more per year for the regional economy by sourcing higher-quality local ice cream that costs the same as national alternatives with less nutritional content.

- Riverside Housing Association saves £46,000 on central heating supplies by working with the regional supply chain.

- Lincolnshire County Council saves over £70,000 per year by working with a local community woodland to provide alternative youth education.

- Liverpool City Council responds to 70 per cent more bulky-waste-removal calls using Bulky Bob's for less money than it previously delivered using a national company.

- Northumberland County Council re-invests £1.5 million per year in regional food suppliers by supplying county schools with fresh food.

Lessons for the future (page 35)
- Ask questions: Question how public sector staff and suppliers alike are incentivised to perform and how these actions relate back to the public body's mission.

- Collaborate and communicate: Find common objectives within your public body, with other public bodies, and with the private enterprises and community organisations that you can or should be working with.

- Start small, start big: You can begin with changing one contract or launching a whole campaign, depending on what mobilises people's interests.

- Change starts with you: Whether you are a policy-maker, a procurement officer, a social entrepreneur, or a concerned resident, you can start the ball rolling.

Recommendations (page 43)
- Question, measure, and improve the local economic impact of public spending.

- Actively promote collaboration within and across public bodies and with local suppliers.

- Redefine costings for contracts, redefine efficiency, and join budgets with other public bodies.

- Change contracting procedure to open the playing field to as many suppliers as possible.

- Remove the layers of jargon and policy that stop passionate individuals from taking action now.

Part 1: Talking the talk

> *"The problem is not necessarily that too little money flows into a neighbourhood. Rather it is what consumers, public services and businesses do with that money. Too often it is spent on services with no local presence, and so immediately leaves the area."*
>
> National Strategy for Neighbourhood Renewal (2000)

> *"... authorities should be open minded about who provides services and they should therefore analyse the markets for services, including in their discussions potential suppliers from all sectors... When the market is weak, authorities are encouraged to see if they can develop the market and help new entrants. This may be especially necessary if small and medium enterprises, social enterprises and voluntary sector bodies are to be encouraged to bid for contracts."*
>
> Competitive Procurement (2002)

> *"The procurement champion, together with other members on the executive, should have prime responsibility for...ensuring equality and sustainability are factored in to the [procurement] strategy and considered at each stage of the procurement process..."*
>
> National Procurement Strategy for Local Government (2003)

> *"NHS organisations are now required to use their role as powerful corporate bodies to act as a good corporate citizen and contribute to public health through their procurement practices – be it through purchasing healthier food; developing local employment schemes; supporting local economies by opening up procurement contracts to local suppliers..."*
>
> Health Development Agency (2005)

Introduction

Key points
- The need for the economic case for promoting regeneration through public spending (page 5).
- How this publication answers the needs of a variety of individuals, including procurement personnel (page 6).
- Why you would bother to read this publication (page 8).

Before someone tells you that your community needs to build a massive shopping development or promote more tourism in order to overcome its fiscal woes, ponder on this figure: In the next fiscal year, the UK public sector expects to spend £125 billion on goods and services.[1] If UK public bodies managed to steer just 10 per cent more of their everyday spending on goods and services into the country's most disadvantaged areas, this would amount to £12.5 billion of income injected into those areas, *in just one year*.

That injection of £12.5 billion equates to more than *17 times* the £725 million allocated annually to the two principle UK regeneration programmes, Neighbourhood Renewal Fund and New Deal for Communities.[2] Every community in the UK, no matter what shape or size, has the ability to develop a strong local economy using the resources it already possesses.

---

1 This figure comes from *Securing the Future: The UK Government Sustainable Development Strategy* (London: HM Government, March 2005). Using other sources, we can find specific breakdowns for part of this figure. Local government spends £40 billion per year; central government spends £13 billion per year; and the NHS spends £15 billion per year. Sources for these figures are, respectively, *National Procurement Strategy for Local Government* (London: ODPM, 2003), Office of Government Commerce website (www.194.128.65.97/whatGovBuys.asp), and Department of Health website (www.advisorybodies.doh.gov.uk/hitf/hitf20031.htm).

2 This figure comes from the ODPM Neighbourhood Renewal Unit website, www.neighbourhood.gov.uk/page.asp?id=10. In Scotland, Communities Scotland expects to spend £110 million on regeneration in financial year 2005–2006.

Policy-makers and practitioners alike have not maximised the opportunity to promote regeneration through public spending. Public spending, particularly procurement, is treated as a mechanistic operation rather than as a creative strategy for achieving multiple objectives.

This publication challenges the belief that public spending and regeneration can be accomplished separately and demonstrates what the UK could look like if public spending achieved multiple objectives through the public procurement process. Evidence comes from public bodies who are *currently* achieving multiple objectives that reduce poverty, promote social inclusion, and ultimately save money for the public purse. These solutions maintain quality, price competitiveness, and conform to legal requirements.

Why this publication

Public procurement has gradually risen up the ranks of the policy agenda in the last few years. Procurement used to be the public sector's dull uncle that no one wanted around at Christmas. 'Best Value', 'contract law', 'supply chain performance', and other terms have not traditionally aroused the public's imagination quite as much as GM crops and asylum seekers.

Yet, public procurement is what affects our daily lives. The streets we walk on, the food our children eat in school, and the buses we travel on – the public procurement process in our communities affects all of these. Like the dull uncle at Christmas (who we inevitably find seated next to us), there is simply no way to avoid public procurement.

There is a substantial foundation of guidance, tools, and training available to foster creativity in public procurement; however, much less is happening than could be.

nef asked the question of public bodies and concerned organisations alike: why?

The answer that came back was that there was a need to make the **economic** case. While public sector guidance, such as the *National Procurement Strategy for Local Government*, recommends that public procurement be 'sustainable' (which will be defined later), pound-stretched local authorities, hospitals and schools are measured and rewarded on other targets, such as short-term targets for cash savings.

Despite much discussion about 'joined-up thinking', we live in a world that constantly incentivises disjointed behaviour. Different public bodies (and different departments within public bodies) guard separate budgets and have no stake in each other's spending behaviour. No single public body is measured or rewarded based on the amount of pollution it generates; public bodies cannot even specify pollution targets in contracts. No single public body is measured or rewarded based on the happiness of its constituency, even if this is the end goal.

Instead, local authorities are measured and rewarded based on how cheaply they can obtain units of goods rather than on the whole life costs of those goods. Schools are measured and rewarded based on test scores rather than how fulfilled students feel. Hospitals are measured and rewarded based on throughput of patients, not on how healthy those patients remain after leaving hospital.

This publication does not seek to blame people or organisations. What we are seeking to do is to set out the raft of opportunities that the public sector has *now*. These are opportunities that conform to current legislation, can be undertaken within tight budgets, and produce results that are competitive with and often cheaper than what public bodies are doing already.

Most importantly, these are opportunities to practically promote regeneration in the most disadvantaged areas of the UK. The only way to promote long-term regeneration is to foster local economic linkages that will endure long after regeneration funding dries up. *Public spending for public benefit* seeks to make the case for regeneration-minded public procurement and to demonstrate that more creative approaches *do* pay off.

Who this publication is for

This publication is written to be understood and utilised by anyone who cares about his or her local economy. There are, of course, a few specific audience members out there.

Ultimately, this publication seeks to inspire anyone with a duty for **purchasing and delivering public services or regeneration**. Public bodies organise themselves differently; some have specific departments dedicated to procurement or enterprise support, while others scatter these responsibilities across the organisation. If you work within a public body, delivering any type of public service, or if you work specifically on regeneration issues, this publication is explicitly for you.

Turning public procurement into a tool for regeneration ultimately relies on **procurement leaders and staff**. They are the keystone to making this happen because it is they who deal with procurement issues on a daily basis. This publication looks at procurement across the public sector – central government, local government, schools, hospitals, universities, and housing associations – so anyone involved in public procurement will learn from it.

There are many others in public bodies who will be interested in or lead on this agenda. Sometimes a **councillor** or **local official** will have the inspiration. A **finance manager** may see a way to make money go further. You can use this publication to back up your position when promoting a regeneration-minded strategy to your constituency.

There are a number of publications that already speak to **enterprises** about how to sell to government. There are also several publications that offer guidance to **social enterprises** on selling to government. This publication is aimed at changing the public sector side of the situation. As an enterprise (whether you consider yourself social or otherwise), you can use this publication to help convince local decision-makers as to why they should be working with you more proactively.

This publication also seeks to arm **residents** and **communities** with the evidence they need to persuade their local public sector decision-makers to rethink their actions.

What you will take away from this publication

The top-level objective of *Public spending for public benefit* is to equip every person in a community with the information they need to challenge and change the way we use public purchasing power. This publication will not be a panacea for you, but it will give you sufficient information to change more hearts and minds. After all, we have documented what other public bodies are *already doing* and how these approaches are working. If these public bodies can make it work, so can yours.

Ground rules

Let's set a few grounds rules first, so you know what this publication is and is not about.

Rule #1: Evidence not rhetoric
This publication is grounded in **evidence**. We flag up what other people in the UK are already doing to make the most of their budgets. We can't set out every step in the process because, like your local economy, each situation is unique. But you will feel better equipped to go out and try.

Rule #2: Realistic
This publication is grounded in **reality**. The evidence presented shows you how people with just as much of a shoestring budget and minimal resources as every other person are taking concrete positive steps forward. You will come away with at least one idea for doing something differently.

Rule #3: Money-focused
This publication is about **cold hard cash**. Every case study in this publication points to actions other public bodies are taking to promote social inclusion that are 100 per cent financially sound. These public bodies are purchasing goods and services from highly competitive local alternatives that are also tackling social exclusion and poverty. And sometimes they're doing it for less money than their competitors. While money is not what motivates most of us, public bodies have to perform to financial bottom lines, so this publication uses the language of finance. Now you will be able to explain why procurement needs to change simply because it will save you money.

Rule #4: Legal
Everything discussed in this publication is **legal**. Government bodies involved in legal issues have reviewed every case study in this publication to ensure that the strategies abide by the law. We also take you through why the approaches described are legal so you'll feel more comfortable with the issues. You will be

able to tell anyone who hems and haws about legality that there's a whole lot you *can* do right now.

Rule #5: Understandable

This publication has been written to be **understandable**. Jargon is avoided where possible, but we define a few key jargon words that inevitably come up in conversations about public procurement (including the word 'procurement' itself).

With these rules in mind, we challenge you to rethink the role of public spending and what it can achieve.

Defining jargon

Jargon and vague language simply alienate readers and create confusion about what we are all trying to achieve, so we avoid them where possible. Below are defined the most crucial words and terms that arise in this publication and in procurement literature in general.

Sustainable

At heart, sustainability is about how the economic, social, and environmental parts of our lives interconnect. It's a challenging concept. What this publication means by sustainable, in the instances it arises, is in reference to economic sustainability. In this case, that means maintaining a full and healthy local economy without relying on external grants, such as Objective 1 funding, for the long-term. We refer to economic sustainability to make the point that communities can regenerate themselves using the money that is already circulating within them from daily life.

Procurement

The most important point to remember about procurement is that *procurement does not equal spending*. In the fewest words possible, procurement refers to *obtaining something*. The fundamental challenge to the public sector is to consider this: What are we trying to obtain? The London Borough of Ealing, for instance, issued a contract for a total waste minimisation solution, not simply a contract for refuse collection and another one for recycling. In this instance, the Council was buying an outcome, waste minimisation, with the precise approach to meeting that outcome left up to the contractor. When we refer to procurement, we refer to all the ways in which the public sector obtains goods and services for itself and the constituency it serves. Other words that float around that are covered by procurement include purchasing, public service delivery, back office spending, and frontline services.

Best Value and 'value for money'

Best Value refers specifically to a legal framework developed under the Local Government Act 1999 and Local Government in Scotland Act 2003 and defined under *Government Accounting* as "the optimum combination of whole-life cost and quality (or fitness for purpose) to meet the user's requirement".[3] Only local government is required to use Best Value to assess contract bids. In short, the Best Value process requires local government to consult with others on how to design and implement services, to review how to make improvements, and to develop targets to evaluate progress. An associated term, 'value for money', is a British phrase that has achieved ubiquity in the public sector, sometimes abbreviated as VfM, but still legally ambiguous.

Efficiency

Efficiency is another term with multiple and often conflicting interpretations. Efficiency can only be defined with reference to what we are trying to conserve or to better achieve. Very strictly speaking, efficiency generally refers to the ratio between what we put in and what we get out. We are more familiar with, for example, energy efficient refrigerators that use less electricity to operate at the same capacity. When it comes to public procurement, we often talk about efficiency in terms of short-term economic costs – the price of a contract and per-unit price. This publication likewise refers to efficiency in terms of money because that is the world in which we all operate. It extends that definition, however, to consider the long-term and other economic factors beyond the price of a contract.

Aggregation

Aggregation is about putting together disconnected parts into a more cohesive whole that achieves more than the two parts could achieve separately. Aggregation *does not* simply mean grouping as much as you can under one contract and getting the cheapest price per unit. One specific point about aggregation is aggregation of *demand* versus aggregation of *supply*. Aggregation of demand means looking at how an organisation procures various goods and services and how these could be joined up more strategically. Aggregation of supply means issuing a contract to one large contractor, rather than allowing separate contractors to bid for different parts of it.

---

3   *Government Accounting 2000*, (London: Office of Government Commerce).

Social enterprise

All social enterprises share an enterprising business-based approach to achieving social and environmental aims. While this publication is not focused exclusively on the use of social enterprises to deliver public contracts, in practice many of the case studies involve social enterprises. In short, social enterprises are businesses trading for a social and/or environmental purpose. Well known examples include *The Big Issue*, Cafédirect and Jamie Oliver's restaurant *Fifteen*. There are several thousand more social enterprises in the UK operating across a wide range of industries and sectors, from social care and recycling to fair-trade and farmers' markets. The social enterprise sector is extremely diverse, encompassing co-operatives, development trusts, community enterprises, housing associations, football supporter's trusts, and leisure trusts.

Local

What is local? It is a question that plagues anyone dealing with regeneration. We all define local for ourselves. The easiest answer is whatever you consider to be your local area is your local area. For the case studies in this publication, local refers to whatever way in which the relevant organisation conceived its local area. We do not seek to challenge what truly constitutes local, preferring to let people use whatever definition inspires them to take action.

Regeneration

Regeneration is the oft-used shorthand word for 'improving a community'. Regeneration literally refers to the process of giving new life or energy and is commonly used with reference to disadvantaged communities. You may see words like economic development, revitalisation, or renewal. They all have the same connotation.

Public spending for public benefit

Key points
- Challenges the reader to consider what we are trying to buy (page 14).
- Highlights the reasons why public bodies are supposed to be achieving regeneration aims through mainstream spending (page 14).
- Offers some innovative ways to alter targets and goal posts when it comes to public contracts (page 16).
- Demonstrates some of the ways that not taking a more strategic course of action now will incur costs later (page 17).
- Highlights ways to 'join up' budgets in a way that reflects real costs (page 19).
- Picks apart the differences between developing local solutions and isolationism (page 21).
- Draws out the historical trends in the public sector's attempts to 'bend mainstream funding' (page 22).

Public spending strategies can deliver the goods and services a community needs *plus* achieve regeneration aims for the same or less money than we are spending now. How is this possible?

Two reasons: first, developing local solutions to public service delivery keeps money circulating in the local economy by fostering local economic linkages, which are critical to long-term regeneration; second, the process of developing local solutions raises capacity and expertise of local people and enterprises, making them more competitive as a whole.

If the public sector delivered school meals or home renovations or recycling services through *proactive* collaboration with disadvantaged communities, then the quality of life in these areas would increase, and the need for dedicated regeneration spending would decrease. Yes, the key word is *proactive*. It's not going to happen without effort; however, the consequence of inaction now is far worse.

The UK currently spends £725 million each year on regeneration programmes[4] dedicated to promoting social inclusion, yet income inequalities have either remained the same or *increased* in the last 20 years.[5] The UK will need to rethink how it delivers all public services in order to avoid needing to spend ever-greater sums to achieve change.

What are we buying?

The straightforward answer is that the aim of public spending, particularly for public service delivery, is to maintain happy and healthy communities. When phrased in such a way, public procurement turns into a highly strategic and creative business.

Why has the role of procurement been relegated to the role of the dull uncle at the Christmas table?

Over the years, the public sector has divorced procurement from the other functions of public bodies. Legislation around procurement has added a hefty and labyrinthine set of regulations seeking to set out the proper legal process. Consequently, public procurement has become a profession that focuses on minimising risk at the expense of maximising benefits.

But it doesn't have to be this way. The UK public sector spends far more on mainstream public goods and services than it does on earmarked regeneration programmes. What if we could turn all of this money into a vehicle for regeneration?

The regeneration mandate

Achieving regeneration through mainstream public spending is not a far-off ideal; the public sector is already required to do so. As laid out by the *National Procurement Strategy for Local Government*, for instance, local authorities are required to "use procurement to help deliver corporate objectives including the

---

4 ODPM Neighbourhood Renewal Unit, www.neighbourhood.gov.uk/page.asp?id=10

5 Goodman A and Webb S (1994) *For Richer, For Poorer*, IFS Commentary no 42 (London: IFS). It should also be noted that until 2005, UK government spent approximately £3 billion per year on regeneration, which includes spending via the Single Regeneration Budget (SRB).

economic, social and environmental objectives set out in the community plan."[6] NHS organisations are now, "required to use their role as powerful corporate bodies to act as a good corporate citizen and contribute to public health through their procurement practices – be it through purchasing healthier food; developing local employment schemes; supporting local economies by opening up procurement contracts to local supplier".[7]

In addition, local authorities are asked to produce corporate procurement strategies that demonstrate how the council will achieve its corporate goals through procurement, and this strategy must also address "the relationship of procurement to the community plan, workforce issues, diversity and equality and sustainability," and "how the council will encourage a diverse and competitive supply market, including small firms, social enterprises, ethnic minority businesses and voluntary and community sector suppliers."[8] Councils are also expected to sign the forthcoming national concordat for small- and medium-sized enterprises (SMEs) that commits councils to involving SMEs in the public procurement process. This concordat arises from the acknowledgment of the crucial role that SMEs play in maintaining a healthy local economy.

Following from commitments raised in the *Choosing Health White Paper*,[9] the Sustainable Development Commission is working with the Department of Health to develop a self-assessment tool for NHS organisations to evaluate how their operations contribute to their local economies, communities, and the environment.[10]

Public bodies also control regeneration spending itself. Even though money may be earmarked for spending under a regeneration initiative, it is subject to EU procurement rules. For this reason, public bodies controlling regeneration spending often treat spending in regeneration areas as straightforward contracts rather than as part of the regeneration process.

A New Deal for Communities (NDC) area, for instance, may determine that building or renovating a community hall will be key to kick-starting the

---

6 Office of the Deputy Prime Minister (2003) *National Procurement Strategy for Local Government* (London: ODPM).

7 Health Development Agency (2005) *Making the case for sustainable procurement: the NHS as a good corporate citizen* (London: Health Development Agency).

8 ODPM (2003) op. cit.

9 Department of Health (2004) *Choosing Health White Paper: making healthier choices easier* (London: Department of Health).

10 The link between the local economy, the environment, and health is based on considerable evidence. For a summary of these issues, see Dalhgren G and Whitehead M (1991) *Policies and strategies to promote social equity in health* (Stockholm: Institute of Futures Studies).

regeneration process. The *presence* of the community hall is considered to be the endpoint, rather than the *process* through which it is created and *how* it is used once built. The result, with which we are all very familiar, is a beautiful building that subsequently falls into disuse because the surrounding local economy is no better off than it was before the community hall was built.

Even in multi-agency regeneration initiatives, public bodies usually hold the purse strings. All regeneration areas have Local Strategic Partnerships (LSPs), a group of individuals representing all interested parties in the area. While the LSPs are expected to make joint decisions, the public body, usually the local authority in the area, still holds the budget. For this reason, regeneration programmes are just as much a part of the public sector budget as everyday goods and services.

Given the mandate to achieve regeneration aims through procurement, as well as the direct involvement of public bodies in regeneration initiatives, there is every reason for those responsible for public spending to link their strategies to whatever regeneration arms exist within their organisation or community.

After Northumberland County Council's procurement team measured the impact their department had on the local economy, subsequent meetings with the regeneration team found a central focal point. Both teams found that, even though they worked in different departments that had not previously worked together, they were both ultimately seeking to achieve the same goals.

Setting the right targets

It is all too easy for us to fall back on jargon when discussing what the aims of procurement are. We are prone to use words like: value for money, competitive price, and efficiency. But what are we really trying to buy?

When explaining why the London Borough of Ealing awarded a massive waste and recycling contract to the apparent underdog (they were also the cheapest bidder), Earl McKenzie explained, "The other tenders had strengths but did not stretch or innovate to the extent required by Ealing at a time of root and branch organisational change. ECT best demonstrated understanding of the integrated nature of the contract, which is not a traditional set of separates but is led by recycling and waste; ECT understands waste minimisation, which is what 60 per cent of the contract is really about." In other words, the Council was buying waste minimisation as an end point. The path towards waste minimisation would entail a changing combination of refuse collection, kerbside recycling, recyclable reclamation, and landfill management; it's up to the contractor how to best deliver that result.

Let's look at an example involving heating services in France that has operated for years:

> Ten million buildings in metropolitan France have long been heated by chauffagistes [professionals who provide heating]; *in 1995, 160 firms in this business employed 28,000 professionals. Rather than selling raw energy in the form of oil, gas, or electricity – none of which is what the customer really wants, namely warmth – these firms contract to keep a client's floorspace within a certain temperature range during certain hours at a certain cost. They can convert your furnace to gas, make your heating system more efficient, or even insulate your building. They're paid for results – warmth – not for how they do it or how much of what inputs they use to do it. The less energy and materials they use – the more efficient they are – the more money they make.*[11]

In this case, what is being procured is the assurance that a building will be maintained at a certain temperature, which is ultimately all that any of the building occupants care about. With every penny we spend, we should ask ourselves this question: What are we really trying to buy here? Whatever the answer is, that is what the contract should in fact be for. In case your gut reaction is, 'but EU or World Trade Organisation (WTO) legislation will never tolerate that?!' be aware that EU and WTO legislation governs the *process* you use to procure; what you choose to buy is completely up to you.

The hunt for savings

You get what you pay for. We remember a parent uttering those words when we were children. Perhaps in an 'I told you so' manner after purchasing a really inexpensive shirt that subsequently fell apart. This publication will not explore production and consumption issues. What we will point out is the many ways that we do in fact get what we pay for, and cheap products beget expensive consequences.

The cost of unhealthy economies

We risk not promoting regeneration of the local economy at our peril. A number of analyses are adding to the growing evidence base that shows the opportunity cost of not promoting healthy economies. The Wanless Report for the Department of Health, *Securing our future health*, pointed to a number of connections between healthy economies and healthy people, or in other words, the link between socio-economic inequality and health inequality.[12] It cites, for instance, that workplace absence, often caused by poor health, costs British businesses £11 billion per year.[13] The report anticipates that the failure to address the root causes of poor health (in the form of people seeking treatment) will result in

---

11   Hawken P, Lovins A and Lovins LH (1999) *Natural Capitalism* (New York: Little, Brown and Company).
12   Wanless D (2002) *Securing our Future Health: Taking a Long-Term View* (London: HM Treasury).

almost a trebling of spending on health between now and 2022. There are many other findings relating health and economics.[14] For instance:

- Mental health problems are estimated to cost the UK £77 billion per year due to the costs of care, economic losses and premature death.[15]

- Children who are diagnosed at age 10 with one of three levels of anti-social behaviour cost public services 10 times as much as those without problems.[16]

- In short, we pay for throwing money at the symptoms and not the cause. The numbers are there, but we seem to choose to ignore them.

Additionally, ensuring the viability of the local economy now will yield benefits for years to come. A study by Caroline Cranbrook of the Council for the Protection of Rural England looked at the evolution of a Suffolk pig farmer who started off by selling high-quality hams and bacon to nearby village shops. Over a number of years, his business grew to supplying 35 local outlets, as well as others outside the region. He said it would have been impossible to start and sustain this successful business if there had been no village shops to which he could sell his products when he first started his business.[17]

Barry Mitchell of Northumberland County Council represents many people's concern over the decreasing choice in the market and the need to think long-term about the regional supply chain: "Working with regional suppliers can seem less important now because we do have choices. But if we don't work with regional suppliers now, they may not exist in a few years, and then we will be stuck with just a few national players. And then we won't have any choices left." For Barry, even maintaining the current regional supply base in today's highly competitive environment is an important achievement.

The local ecology of enterprise in your area is therefore crucial to preserve: if we don't foster the development of SMEs, then we are left only with a few larger

---

13 Confederation of British Industry (2001) *Pulling Together* (Newmarket: Confederation of British Industry).

14 Wanless op. cit.

15 ODPM (2004) *Breaking the Cycle: Taking stock of progress and priorities for the future* (London: ODPM).

16 Scott S, Knapp M, Henderson J and Maughan B (2001) 'Financial cost of social exclusion: follow-up study of antisocial children into adulthood' *British Medical Journal*, 323:191-194 (London: BMJ Publishing Group).

17 Cranbrook C (1998) *Food Webs* (London: Council for the Protection of Rural England).

businesses that will face less competition, a reduced need to innovate, and ultimately the consumer will suffer.

Accounting for all spending

We all know about the connection between, for example, food and health. Taking action is hard because we live in a world where we have separate budgets, responsibilities, and targets. We see the connections but find it difficult to act on them. In a recent letter from Lord Whitty to regional public bodies, he comments:

> *Of particular concern is evidence that some public sector bodies are implementing the [Gershon[18]] Review by cutting the cost of their procurement without properly weighing up the effect on other operations within their own organisations or on the public sector as a whole. For example, cutting budgets for the procurement of food and catering where this results in the provision of less healthy and nutritious food can result in more spending by the NHS [National Health Service] on obesity and heart disease etc. That's not realising long-term benefits.*[19]

This is a crucial point, and no one would debate the validity of Lord Whitty's words. The reality, however, is that the NHS and the schools in your community do not share budgets. If a school wants to spend more on food to promote health, there is no ready and apparent way for the NHS to allocate some of its money to the school, acknowledging that this money will be savings later on.[20]

A number of local authorities, many in the case studies in Part 2, have attempted to tear down budget barriers by using their enterprise support funds to develop local businesses and capacity. Sheffield City Council used regeneration funds to develop a social enterprise, Sheffield Rebuild, to meet growing construction needs in a way that also promoted local economic development. Sheffield City Council now uses Sheffield Rebuild as one of its construction suppliers, and Sheffield Rebuild now operates an annual turnover of £6 million and employs 160 people. Gloucestershire County Council started up a foster care agency to meet children's needs on a grant of £70,000 in 1999. The market need was well spotted, and the foster care agency, Community Foster Care, now operates an annual turnover of £1 million and employs 40 carers.

---

18 The quotation refers to Gershon P (2004), *Releasing resources to the front line*, (London: HM Treasury). Scotland plans to unveil similar savings targets under the Efficient Government Plan.

19 Letter from Lord Larry Whitty, Minister for Food, Farming and Sustainable Energy, 3 December 2004, Defra website www.defra.gov.uk/farm/sustain/procurement/pdf/lwhitty-laletter.pdf

20 The ODPM is currently piloting 'Local Area Agreements', for which all of the public bodies in one geographic area share a pooled budget. Results are due in 2006.

Redefining efficiency

With the above in mind, the notion of efficiency takes a different shape. We are more familiar with the notion of environmental efficiency, such as a new refrigerator that keeps food fresh using less energy, or a well-insulated home that requires less energy to heat and to cool it.

When it comes to procurement, this publication is trying to put some meat on the bones of what we mean by economic efficiency: squeezing out as much value as we can from every penny we spend. Sheffield City Council now has a competitive local construction company, which has helped to keep costs more affordable as the cost of construction nationally rises. Gloucestershire County Council now saves more money through its use of Community Foster Care than it ever spent on start-up funding.

Still, you may feel that developing new suppliers is the exact *opposite* of what local public bodies are trying to do right now. If anything, the move is towards reducing and consolidating suppliers, even closing the approved supplier list to discourage new entrants. The case studies in Part 2 demonstrate how halting and reversing this process is key to promoting regeneration; they also demonstrate that an approach to consolidation has cost some public bodies more money than using an array of businesses.

Reducing and consolidating suppliers works for goods and services that are uniform and specialised, such as electromagnetic scanning equipment.[21] When it comes to other services, however, using the logic of economies of scale means applying a bog standard or cookie-cutter model to every community.

As many of the public bodies in the case studies found, the one-size-fits-all approach works when you live in a 'normal' community but costs more or fails to meet community needs when you fall outside of the norm. In Wales, for instance, the public bodies devised their own private car hire framework contract for Wales because the previous UK-wide contract, while cheaper for many English public bodies, came out dearer for Wales. The leaders of the Cornwall Food Programme developed local suppliers because the suppliers operating under national framework contracts charged extra for delivering food to Cornwall (referred to as 'non-mainland Britain' by one supplier!).

---

21 Even for specialised medical technology, though, there are initiatives to develop local solutions. ZAB in Germany (ZukunftsAgentur Brandenburg) has developed a strong local network to supply sophisticated medical equipment to hospitals in the area. For more information, see www.zab-brandenburg.de.

Local solutions versus isolationism

One important distinction is required: this publication is not advocating isolationism, rather local solutions for local problems. What's the difference?

First, humans are innate problem-solvers. Every day, we encounter a number of challenges, small and large, that we attempt to solve. Solving problems is a passion that drives our daily lives. This publication documents how people are challenging the notion that solving problems should be left to the 'experts' and instead are finding their own solutions using the resources they have. All public bodies should want to foster creativity and innovation in their local area.

Second, this publication is about promoting *regeneration* through procurement. So the strategies advocated are primarily for disadvantaged communities where getting more money circulating locally is a challenge. If you live in a wealthier community, we advocate you partner with nearby disadvantaged communities to find solutions together.

Third, it is true that if every community in the UK blindly attempted to move all of its spending to the local economy, then this would be to the detriment of everyone. The connections between local economies promote not only economic success but also cultural exchange and innovation. The concern that we are suddenly going to plunge into a British turf war, however, is unfounded. The world in which every public body in the UK is pursuing a large-scale strategy to promote local money flows is Point C. We are currently at Point A, where few public bodies are considering or feel able to find ways to use more of their mainstream spending to achieve regeneration aims. (If you doubt this, then your challenge is to ask your colleagues what the current economic impact of their budget is.) Getting some public bodies to that position is Point B. It is useful to have the long-term outcome on the radar, but not at the risk of discouraging public bodies from trying to take some action first.

Fourth, this publication puts forward a series of case studies that demonstrates the manifold benefits of working to promote real solutions to local problems. In Cornwall, for instance, the flexibility and shared interest of the locally based cheese company enabled the Cornwall Food Programme to find a source of higher quality yet lower cost cheese for hospital patients. In Lincolnshire, the County Council and a local community woodland were able to devise unconventional youth education with nationally renowned success rates. Such solutions are in everyone's interest.

These solutions do not necessarily need to come from businesses based in the local economy; however, the experience of those in the case studies and elsewhere is that locally based enterprises have a stake in the local economy and are therefore more willing to collaborate with the public sector on finding solutions to local problems. Public bodies can work with non-local businesses to develop solutions to local problems as well. In the case of Sheffield City Council, the Council capitalised on the capacity and know-how of larger businesses to transfer that knowledge to local enterprises.

Finally, there are always underserved markets, market gaps, or niches that can be developed. A key issue raised in the 2002 Audit Commission *Competitive Procurement* report was that:

> "...authorities should be open minded about who provides services and they should therefore analyse the markets for services, including in their discussions potential suppliers from all sectors. This market analysis can also provide new ideas for alternative service design. When the market is weak, authorities are encouraged to see if they can develop the market and help new entrants. This may be especially necessary if small and medium enterprises, social enterprises and voluntary sector bodies are to be encouraged to bid for contracts."[22]

Only those in the local area will possess an intimate understanding of what these needs are, so they are best placed to participate in the development of a solution. In Gloucestershire, it was the observation of a market gap in certain types of foster care provision that motivated the local authority and others in the community to set up a locally based social enterprise to meet that need. In the London neighbourhood of Ealing, a locally based social enterprise pioneered the first ever kitchen waste recycling scheme in the UK and developed a GIS system for determining recycling habits.

These innovations and market developments have benefited the public sector in the form of better value and quality, and local people benefit from better services.

Old is new again

Read the following quotation and guess what policy document it came from:

> "The urban studies of recent years have shown that urban problems cannot be tackled effectively on a piecemeal basis. The problems interlock: education, for example, is affected by social conditions which in turn are affected by housing and by employment. The best results are likely to be achieved through a unified approach in which the different activities

---

[22] The Audit Commission (2002) *Competitive Procurement: learning from audit inspection and research* (London: Audit Commission Publications).

and services of government are brought together. Concerted action should have a greater impact. It should lead to a more efficient use of resources by avoiding duplication or conflicts of effort, and it ought to be more sensitive to the needs of the public who do not see problems in departmental or agency terms."[23]

Interlocking problems, concerted action, efficient use of resources – sounds familiar, right? The quotation above comes from the 1977 Urban White Paper, *Policy for the Inner Cities*. This was the first major document to outline the need to 'bend mainstream spending', which is now of course a popular phrase to describe what this publication sets out: using mainstream spending to achieve regeneration. The White Paper was innovative in laying out the need for central and local government to consider how mainstream spending could regenerate the UK's inner cities and specified housing as one specific area where the public sector should incorporate this agenda.

Beyond the genesis of several national programmes, such as the Urban Programme, 'bending mainstream programmes' has remained elusive. The Office of the Deputy Prime Minister's Neighbourhood Renewal Unit (NRU) acknowledges that, while the current 'bend the spend' programme is grounded in the 1977 Urban White Paper, "In practice, however, the evidence – from the most recent experience as well as that of the past thirty years – is that it has proved extremely difficult to enforce such 'bending'."[24] The NRU goes onto cite 'short-termism' and 'organisational inflexibility' as the two major causes for the failure to achieve this vision. What has happened?

Among the many bold statements of the 1977 Urban White Paper, the policy document identifies several other actions necessary to truly bend mainstream programmes. First, the White Paper identifies the need for local government to draw on the interests and energy of local residents:

"Involving local people is both a necessary means to the regeneration of the inner areas and an end in its own right. Public authorities need to draw on the ideas of local residents, to discover their priorities and enable them to play a practical part in reviving their areas. Self-help is important and so is community effort."[25]

---

23 Urban White Paper (1977) *Policy for the Inner Cities* (London: Her Majesty's Stationery Office).

24 OPDM (2002) *How to influence the mainstream*, ODPM website www.renewal.net

25 Urban White Paper, op. cit.

The White Paper then sets out a series of best practice solutions known at that time:

> "Local authorities, for their part, can do a great deal to redirect their policies to give greater assistance to inner areas and to bring about a more co-ordinated approach. There is scope for making better use of resources and for pursuing policies of positive discrimination. There are many fields where the need is for a change in policies, including regulatory policies, so that the best does not become the enemy of the good. For example:
>
> (a) some local authorities, in their town planning work, have in recent years shown much more tolerance of 'non-conforming users' to ensure that existing businesses are not displaced by redevelopment; where a move is absolutely essential, authorities should make certain that suitable alternative arrangements are made for relocation in the area;
>
> (b) the delivery of different social services might in some instances be co-ordinated more effectively at the local level; this would particularly benefit those in special need, for example, the aged, the handicapped [sic] and the under-fives;
>
> (c) housing policies need to take account of employment opportunities; local authority tenants can be given greater responsibility in the running of their estates; steps can be taken to improve housing mobility."

The White Paper also recommends that, "Local authorities can do much to improve employment prospects by looking after existing firms, including small businesses, and encouraging new enterprises."

The astounding similarities between current policy and the 1977 Urban White Paper illustrate how not only our goals but also the challenges we face in achieving those goals have been constant over decades. The issue, then and now, is not that it is economically unviable to 'bend mainstream spending'. The challenge has remained, as the NRU points out, short-termism and organisational inflexibility. There is only so much you can do about that right now. What you can do, however, is use the evidence in this publication to begin taking some action to 'bend mainstream spending'.

Valuing the local economy

Key points
- The local economy is like a leaky bucket, with money entering, being exchanged, and leaking out (page 26).

- The only way to keep the bucket full is to ensure there is a steady stream of water or to plug the leaks (page 26).

- The amount of income generated for the local economy is called the 'multiplier effect' (page 27).

- You can quantify how much your spending impacts on the local economy using **nef**'s LM3 tool (page 29).

- You can spend less money but generate more income for your local economy by promoting local economic linkages (page 31).

- Developing local economic linkages produces other economic benefits that you can measure (page 31).

- You can promote the local economy legally (page 33).

What is the local economy worth to you? It's not an answer any of us can easily put a price tag on. What is it worth to you to have a cashpoint within walking distance? Or healthy, safe food delivered to your door? What is it worth to you to have employment opportunities that you actually want? None of us can truly place a cash figure on the options that enable us to lead a happy, fulfilling life. Nevertheless, the public sector budgeting process requires price tags. In Part 2, we draw on a set of case studies to document in quantitative terms why the local economy matters. In other words, we can't afford *not* to think about the people and businesses that comprise our local economy.

The regeneration game

As acknowledged by the Government's *National Strategy for Neighbourhood Renewal*, which set the tone for many regeneration programmes operating in the UK at this moment, "The problem is not necessarily that too little money flows into a neighbourhood. Rather it is what consumers, public services and businesses do with that money. Too often it is spent on services with no local presence, and so immediately leaves the area."[26] These words are as true today as they have been for the past several decades of targeted regeneration spending.

For many years, the proposed solution for regenerating urban and rural areas has been to attract more money into them, whether it is in the form of tourism, agriculture, corporate relocations, or other forms of inward investment. This publication and the case studies in Part 2 showcase a different strategy: regenerating the local economy from within the community by taking advantage of the resources that communities *already possess*.

The leaky bucket

One way to think about the local economy is like a leaky bucket. A full bucket represents a healthy local economy, where there are enough resources for everyone. Money enters your local economy just like pouring water into a bucket. Your local economy sees money enter it through tourism spending, welfare benefits, and earnings from residents and businesses based in the community. There are leaks in the bucket, however, similar to the way we all spend money outside of our local economy. We spend money on taxes, energy, waste, and all the goods and services we purchase from elsewhere.

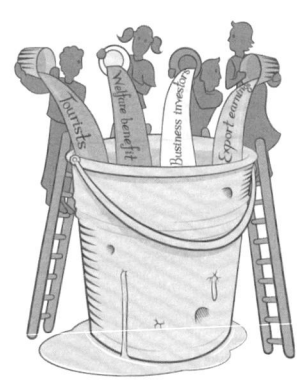

There are two ways to keep the bucket full: pour more water into it or plug the leaks to stop the water from flowing out. As identified by the *National Strategy for Neighbourhood Renewal* and many other analyses, our gut instinct is to pour more water into the bucket, often because that is much easier to do than to find ways to plug the leaks. Of course, that works as long as we have an endless source of water, which we don't. The case studies in Part 2 demonstrate how many public bodies across the UK are taking action to plug the leaks. They are finding ways to transform their current spending into an agent for regeneration.

---

26 Social Exclusion Unit (2000) *National Strategy for Neighbourhood Renewal: a framework for consultation* (London: Cabinet Office).

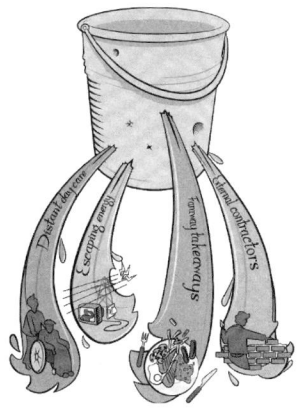

Rather than, for example, spend money for a construction project and then spend money later on job training for long-term unemployed people, these public bodies are combining the two to achieve multiple objectives. It does take work, but in every one of the case studies the work has paid off.

We have summarised the concept of the leaky bucket, but you can find more detailed explanation in *Plugging the Leaks*, available on the **nef** website.[27]

The multiplier effect

There's a way to quantify what happens to water that enters your bucket (or money that enters your local economy), and it's captured in an economics concept known as the 'multiplier effect'.

Developed by John Maynard Keynes in collaboration with other economists in the early twentieth century, the multiplier has been used in every sphere of policy-making since that time. The theory behind the multiplier effect, like all economics concepts, is not without contention; however, it is a widely accepted model that is still in use today when producing evaluations of the economic impact of investments, initiatives, and trade.

The gist is this: economies are comprised of money entering, being exchanged, and leaving. The more people spend money on other people and businesses in their local economy, the more income is generated for people in that local economy. This makes sense if you think of it this way: each time you earn money, it is like new money for you; it doesn't matter where that money comes from. The more income that is generated in your local economy, the higher the multiplier effect.

Let's look at a fictitious comparison to make the point clear. Overleaf you'll see two graphs. The top graph represents the multiplier effect for Localton, where everyone magically spends 80 per cent of his or her income locally. The bottom graph represents the multiplier effect for Leakyville, where everyone magically spends 20 per cent of his or her income locally. In both Localton and Leakyville, we start off with £100 entering the locally economy. In Localton, that person spends 80 per cent of her £100 locally (£80). The next person spends

---

27 Ward B and Lewis J (2002) *Plugging the Leaks* (London: **nef**) www.neweconomics.org

Income generated by the local multiplier effect

Income generated in Localton
Everone spends 80% of their income locally

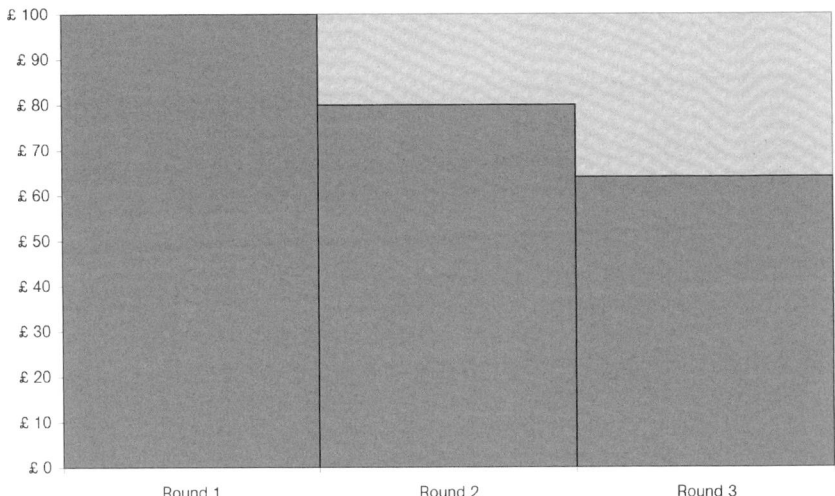

Income generated in Leakyville
Everyone spends 20% of their income locally

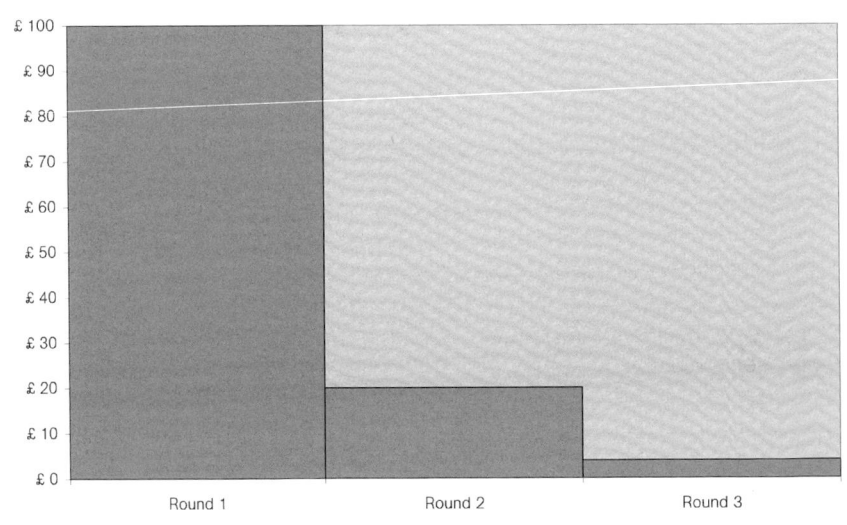

80 per cent of his £80 of income locally (£64), and so on. In contrast, the person receiving £100 in Leakyville spends 20 per cent of his income locally (£20). The next person spends 20 per cent of her income locally (£4), and so on. The dark grey area represents the multiplier effect in each place. You can see what a difference in income arises between Localton and Leakyville.

No local economy looks like either of these extremes, but there are many places, often disadvantaged areas with few local shops or job opportunities, where most of the money that enters the local economy immediately leaves. For example, an American study found that three-quarters of the money spent by the federal government on Native American reservations leaves the community within 48 hours.[28] A methodology used in the USA looks at a community the way an accountant looks at a business, creating a 'community balance sheet'. A study of the Camden neighbourhood in Minneapolis found that the 10,833 households in the neighbourhood earned $340 million per year but spent $260 million (over three-quarters!) of that income outside the community.[29] For both the Native American reservation and the Camden neighbourhood, such a level of leakiness means that the inhabitants must continue to bring money in from outside in order to sustain themselves.

You understand this concept intuitively; however, you may just not have known that there was a word for it!

Economic evaluation in the case studies and Local Multiplier 3 (LM3)

One goal of this publication is to start quantifying the value of the approaches highlighted in the case studies. By quantifying value, we can see how developing local solutions is not only politically appealing but, more importantly, economically advantageous.

Some of the case studies used a specific tool to evaluate their economic impact, called Local Multiplier 3 (LM3). **nef** developed this measuring tool in 2002 as a response to the need for people to be able to evaluate their economic impact in a simple yet robust manner.

The name indicates how the tool works. First, LM3 is based on the Keynesian multiplier we discussed in the previous section. **nef** adapted the multiplier for use at the local level. This is an important distinction between the way Keynes envisioned the multiplier, as he only used it at the national or regional level. The

---

28 Shuman MH, 'Amazing Shrinking Machines: Local Economies are Thriving Alternatives to Globalism' *New Village Journal*, Issue 2 (Oakland, CA: New Village Press) www.newvillage.net/Journal/Issue2/2amazing.html, accessed June 2005

29 Meter K (1995) *Camden Community Income Statement and Balance Sheet*, (Minneapolis: Crossroads Resource Center).

'3' comes from the fact that we stop measuring after three 'rounds' of spending rather than continue onwards. This is where the bulk of spending takes place, and it also becomes burdensome to keep tracking beyond this point.

The LM3 for the contracts measured in the case studies works like this:

- Start with the original source of income, which is the budget that the public body has to spend on a particular service (Round 1).

- Then look at how that public body spends its budget, which is sometimes just the contract itself but also could include training or grant funding (Round 2) – the contractor might be where all the money is spent.

- Then look at how the recipients of that money spend it in a defined local area (e.g. parish, ward, district, or 30-mile radius) – suppliers, staff, subcontractors, and overhead are typically the principal expenditures (Round 3).

- Finally, run through some quick maths to arrive at the LM3, which tells you how much spending by the organisation impacts the local economy.

A quick example brings this to life. Back in 2002, when **nef** was developing LM3, we worked with North Norfolk District Council on comparing the LM3 for two construction contracts. We used contracts for comparable concrete work, a sea wall constructed by Contractor 1 and a car park constructed by Contractor 2. Since such work requires little specialised labour or materials, it was possible for both contractors to use local labour and supplies for the respective jobs.

Here's what we found:

LM3 for two construction contracts

	Contractor 1	Contractor 2
Round 1	£72,000	£120,000
Round 2	£57,600	£20,400
Round 3	£24,987	£6,768
Total	**£154,587**	**£147,168**
LM3	**2.15**	**1.23**

The LM3 score for each construction contract is calculated by adding up Rounds 1–3 and dividing by Round 1. This gives us a *relative* figure, which means that we know how much income was generated in relation to the original source of income (Round 1).

We found the LM3 for Contractor 1 to be 2.15, while the LM3 for Contractor 2 was 1.23. This means that for every £1 spent with Contractor 1, an additional £1.15 was generated for North Norfolk, while only 23p was generated by Contractor 2.

This application illustrates quite clearly that it is not the *quantity* of money thrown at the local economy but *how* the money then circulates in the local economy after the council spends it. Even though North Norfolk District Council spent nearly twice as much money on the contract for Contractor 2 (£120,000 versus £72,000 paid to Contractor 1), the spending on Contractor 1 actually generated *more* money for the North Norfolk economy!

The reason for the disparity between the two contracts above comes down to **economic linkages**. How connected is your local economy? This is the question you need to ask yourself when thinking of how to regenerate your area for the long run. As the North Norfolk example illustrates, we can pour as much money as we want into disadvantaged neighbourhoods, but unless we build linkages between businesses and people in our local economy, then that money will leak right out again.

Some case studies will refer to the LM3 score if the organisations involved used LM3 to evaluate their impact. Otherwise, we refer to other cash figures. You can find more information on the multiplier effect and using LM3 in **nef**'s how-to handbook, *The Money Trail*, which is available from the **nef** website.[30]

Other ways to rethink economic impact

'Increasing local money flows is nice, but where's the savings?' you ask. Businesses that actively connect up to the local economy do save the public sector money. The money saved is not always so obvious at the time of evaluating and awarding a contract, but, as the case studies in Part 2 demonstrate, there are both immediate and long-term savings generated from rethinking 'value for money'. Questions to ask yourself include:

- Does the company employ or train the very people we're trying to move into employment through other programmes?

- Does the company offer trading discounts to others in the area?

---

30 Sacks J (2003) *The Money Trail* (London: **nef**) www.neweconomics.org

- Does the company make cash or in-kind contributions to the community?

- Does working with this company enable me to access other funding, such as regeneration grants?

- Whom does the company employ or train?

Yes, suppliers can cost more if they work with people who are long-term unemployed, on incapacity benefit, come from disadvantaged communities, or have learning difficulties or mental health problems. These costs are borne elsewhere in the public budget if they are not addressed through such suppliers. For instance, the average Jobseeker's Allowance comes to roughly £2,300 per year.[31] Finding ways to move that person into a job he or she enjoys not only eliminates that cost but also generates income for the public sector in the form of tax and National Insurance (NI) payments. A job that pays £15,000 per year will generate £2,000 in tax and £1,100 in NI each year.

Trading discounts are an indirect way that a company saves money for the local economy. Many local businesses operate trading partnerships, whether structured or tacit, with other businesses in the area. Trading discounts save businesses money that they can pass onto future clients (including the public sector) as well as re-invest into the company.

Many companies make cash or in-kind contributions to the community. We are often led to believe that this is the only way that a company can contribute to a community and we forget that the local economic linkages described in this publication can have a far more powerful impact. Nevertheless, contributions to the community directly offset public spending.

A key advantage many public bodies have had in working with locally based companies, particularly social enterprises, is the ability to leverage that relationship to bring more money into the area. If you are thinking of applying for regeneration funding, business support funding, or any number of grants from the UK or EU, they will ask for proof of previous work with the community. Local authorities that have been able to demonstrate their relationships to local suppliers have traditionally been more successful in accessing this funding.

---

31 JobCentre Plus website,
    www.jobcentreplus.gov.uk/cms.asp?Page=/Home/Customers/WorkingAgeBenefits/497#what

Keeping it legal

'We just can't do this because of EU regulations' is the knee-jerk response of many procurement officers. While EU regulations are in place to prevent procurement officers from awarding contracts to their brothers, there is an awful lot you can do within the law. The most common misconceptions are:

- I can't talk to businesses in my community about doing business with us.
- I can't build social benefits into my contracts.
- I can't break my contract down and award it to multiple companies.
- I can't ask for proof of local economic impact.
- Once the contract is awarded, my job is over.
- If I change parts of the contract during delivery, I must pay more for those changes.
- EU regulations mean that I can only tender for specific services.

All of the above statements, as you have already guessed, are incorrect. The case studies in Part 2 will show that you that you *can*:

- Proactively engage with businesses in your area to boost their chances of being able to compete for public contracts, as well as to improve your local economy in general, as long as you do not give those enterprises an unfair advantage during the procurement process.
- Build a number of social, as well as environmental, benefits into your contracts.
- Divide up contract services into a number of ways, as long as you are breaking down your contract to achieve a better value rather than to avoid EU thresholds.
- Include a requirement for bidders to submit optional, priced proposals for the delivery of community benefits, as long as they are relevant to the contract and the authority's community plan.
- Work with a supplier to develop a local supply chain and employment opportunities to deliver a better service after awarding a contract.

- Work with a supplier to deliver services in the most cost-effective way over the course of service delivery if you structure your contracts to be 'open-book'.[32]

- Determine *what* you as a public body want to tender for, as EU regulations simply specify *how* you must tender for goods and services.

This publication focuses more on the economic value of innovative solutions to public service delivery rather than on the detailed legal issues; however, there are a number of guidance documents that lay out the opportunities that public bodies do have. In particular, *Proactive Procurement* illustrates how public bodies can deliver quality services using the existing legal framework.[33]

---

32 For a brief explanation of the open book approach see: Strategic Partnering Taskforce (2004) *Rethinking Service Delivery*, Volume 5: Making the Partnership a Success (London: ODPM).

33 Cook M and Alcock D (2004) *Proactive Procurement* (Manchester: Co-operatives[UK]).

Lessons for the future

Key points
- **Ask questions**: Don't accept the status quo! Question how public sector staff and suppliers alike are incentivised to perform and how these actions relate back to the public body's mission (page 36).

- **Collaborate and communicate**: Strength in numbers! Find common objectives within your public body, with other public bodies, and with the private enterprises and community organisations that you can or should be working with (page 37).

- **Start small, start big**: Start somewhere! You can begin with changing one contract or launching a whole campaign, depending on what mobilises people's interests (page 39).

- **Rural issues**: All economies are not the same! Rural areas need to take into account working across a more dispersed group of resources (page 41).

- **Change starts with you**: There is a role for everyone! Whether you are a policy-maker, procurement officer, social entrepreneur, or concerned resident, you can start the ball rolling (page 42).

nef's work with public bodies and the advice coming back from those at the forefront of rethinking procurement have generated a few broad lessons. The major lessons learned from the case studies in this publication, alongside other work taking place in the UK are:

Ask questions

Why, why, why? In all of the case studies in this publication, change occurred because someone was willing to challenge the status quo. Why does my organisation require three years' accounts in order for a business to qualify to tender? Have we considered asking local businesses why they choose not to work with us? How are we actually achieving our community plan through procurement spending? The source of tension most often lies in one of three places.

Internal accountability

One of the biggest hurdles in changing the status quo for many of the public bodies in this publication was the internal accountability structure. The procurement staff are paid to get the most for their money for each contract. The social services department staff are paid to deliver the services people expect of them. Fostering a conversation and taking some creative steps with budgeting is in no one's remit. In a lot of the case studies, one person took some action, and once others saw the positive impact of that action, they were willing to have a discussion. In Northumberland, the success of a few people in the procurement department who changed the way the Council delivered its food contract attracted the attention of other departments, and they are now working together. One aim of this publication is provide the evidence needed to kick-start that conversation earlier on in the process.

External accountability

How do you measure success in contracts? What incentives, deliberate and unintended, are built into your contracts? For instance, a recycling contract that pays a flat rate for delivery of recycling services can incentivise the contractor to cut corners in order to make a profit. Requiring the same food items throughout the year rather than letting the contractor deliver food based on seasonality can mean that only national suppliers can compete, and only by sourcing low-quality food from abroad grown out of season.

Many of the successes we showcase relied on a partnership-style approach to contract delivery. London Borough of Ealing and ECT Group have an open-book contract, allowing both organisations to constantly alter services to meet everyone's needs in the best way possible. Lincolnshire County Council and Hill Holt Wood work together on an ongoing basis to develop and adjust the curriculum offered to ensure students' needs are met.

Strategy

One of the best foundations for many of the public bodies taking action was to embed regeneration and economic development goals in various strategic documents. Produced by most public bodies, these strategic documents are often written up and then sit on a shelf.

Don't let this happen! Raise the objectives specified in those documents with colleagues and others, and use the presence of those objectives to help your case. Once you get the ball rolling, also keep those strategic documents in mind. The more you get the idea of regeneration-minded procurement into a public body's strategy, the more people will listen. After a lot of discussion about the importance of the local multiplier effect, Northumberland County Council's finance department has now set a target of switching ten per cent of its spending to local sources over the next three years.

Strategic documentation also ensures that momentum continues even if individual champions move on. A useful strategic resource within local authorities is the overview and scrutiny committee. Introduced as part of the Local Government Act 2000, a local authority can use the overview and scrutiny committee mechanism to review how it can use its strategic procurement framework more effectively. One local authority, for instance, used its committee to assess the role of the voluntary and community sector and its potential for supplying public goods and services.

Collaborate

The key to success in all of the case studies in this publication has been collaboration. Collaboration can mean as little as keeping an open communication channel or as much as partnering on a project. Keeping doors closed, however, raises costs for everyone.

Collaboration with other public bodies

The simplest starting point is to open up communication lines within the public body. This is how Northumberland County Council put procurement onto the regeneration radar and how Sheffield City Council used its regeneration budget to develop a construction service organisation.

In some of the case studies, individuals found allies in other public bodies, sometimes more readily than within their own organisation. Riverside Housing Association's involvement in Fusion 21 is a clear example of how collaboration works to everyone's benefit. By partnering with other registered social landlords (RSLs), Riverside found ways to deliver the same quality for less money. Collaborating with other public bodies enables the individual public bodies to achieve their goals more effectively, fosters learning across organisations, and leads to quality improvement.

Collaboration with the private sector

Many of the case studies demonstrate how collaboration with the private sector is key and beneficial. For Sheffield and Fusion 21, both dealing with construction demand that outstrips supply, the only way to foster local regeneration has been to partner through the private sector. In both instances, the public bodies were able to use the private sector to develop local capacity while meeting short-term targets. A key ingredient in both cases was harnessing the expertise of the private sector while incorporating local capacity building as a criterion for partnership.

In many other initiatives, the public sector has proactively worked with SMEs to find ways to make them fit to compete for contracts. In the North West, for instance, the North West NHS Supplier Bureau is working with SMEs so they can compete for NHS contracts in the region. Support includes tender training delivered by the NHS Purchasing and Supply Agency (PASA) and one-to-one support delivered by Groundwork to enable suppliers to sharpen their health, safety, and environmental management. Support and funding for the initiative comes straight from NHS PASA and the North West Regional Development Agency because they recognise the potential to shift some of the £2.2 billion the NHS spends in the North West each year. A shift of just one per cent of that spending to local suppliers would amount to an injection of £22 million into the North West's local economy.[34]

Collaboration with the community and voluntary sector

There is a strong role for the voluntary and community sector (VCS) in the approaches discussed in this publication. The case studies only partially document this role because much of that work took place beforehand. The VCS has the network, knowledge, and community connections to help a public body turn ideas into action. Note that in the case studies, social enterprises are not considered to be part of the VCS; however, many of them started off as part of the VCS and were able to move into the private sector as they became more established and grew. ECT Group, for instance, started off as a public transport charity. Hill Holt Wood is a community-owned business, which doesn't officially make it part of the VCS, but it delivers much of the same agenda.

Communicate

The lesson from all of the case studies is the role of communication. In all cases, the public body, and consequently the public, benefited from increased communication. Communication in the form of the 'closed loop system' in the Fusion 21 model means that RSLs secure better prices and quality from their supply chain. Communication in the form of the open-book contract between

---

[34] For more information on the North West Supplier Bureau, see www.intend.org. Another project involving the NHS and the private sector is Salford's Health Investment For Tomorrow (SHIFT) programme. The SHIFT programme is a private finance initiative (PFI) for which potential PFI partners were required to demonstrate how they proposed to facilitate local economic development by encouraging local supply chain partners, using social enterprises, committing to local workforce development. For more information on the SHIFT programme, see www.shiftprogramme.co.uk

London Borough of Ealing Council and ECT Group means the Council keeps costs down by working with the contractor on delivering solutions.

There is a tendency in the procurement world to keep one's cards out of view, but the case studies demonstrate that everyone wins when we put our cards on the table for everyone to look at. It is only then that we all know the resources and constraints we are dealing with, and we can begin re-arranging the cards in a way that benefits the public body, the contractor, and ultimately the public.

Start small

Whether it's changing procurement or something else, many of us tend to think big and then feel overwhelmed by the amount we have to do. As many of the case studies demonstrate, you can start small.

For instance, Annette Williams took the reigns of Strategic Procurement Officer at Devon County Council in 2003 with a goal of raising the profile of procurement throughout the Council as a strategic activity. There was tentative support for this work when Annette started but no resource commitments.

Annette used LM3 to evaluate a sampling of Council contracts, such as food, construction and technology. She also undertook a countywide survey of SMEs to understand the opportunities afforded by and barriers faced in working with the Council. In 2004, Annette presented LM3 results alongside the SME survey to demonstrate how strategic procurement activity could contribute to corporate objectives; in this case, local economic development. Using LM3 provided Annette with exactly the type of hard evidence that gets people's attention: results in pounds and pence.

This project was one of the procurement profile-raising exercises that contributed to securing resources for a Corporate Procurement Service, which went live in April 2005. The Corporate Procurement Service emerged from the former Devon Purchasing Office; the name change reflects the transformation at the Council in thinking of procurement as a strategic lever for achieving multiple objectives rather than as a routine operation.

Building on the success of the first LM3 evaluations, the newly-formed Corporate Procurement Service has embarked on other LM3 projects, including the base-lining of all food contracts within the Council (with a value of £6 million) as to their 'local produce' content.

While Devon County Council had been working towards healthier school menus for some time, there had never been focused targets. Using local economic impact as a way to focus everyone's energy, Annette has established, as a first step, an early target of increasing locally produced food within the Council's supply chain by 10 per cent. In addition to considering the health and educational benefits of school meals sourcing, the Corporate Procurement Service will be using LM3 to measure the impact on the local economy before and after the changes are made.

Contracts

An easy starting point is a contract. This is how Northumberland County Council focused its efforts. With long-term contracts in place, most public bodies cannot address every contract right away, but they can start with whatever is coming up in that year. There are many small changes you can make depending on how much time you have available. The case studies illustrate the range of options: proactively discussing opportunities with regional businesses, connecting regional businesses to support organisations, changing the tendering specifications to more closely reflect what you want to buy, changing the tendering process to open up the playing field, etc.

Even if you fail to make any changes in your first attempt, you will learn from that experience and apply that knowledge to the next one. If you do see an impact, then you can use those results to secure more commitment from your organisation.

Subcontractors

Since so many public contracts are long-term, enduring anywhere from two to twenty years, public bodies have to work within the current contract constraints. This means working with the contractor to find ways to improve the supply chain that also regenerate your local economy. In some cases, as in Sheffield, there simply isn't the capacity to deliver the contract, so the public body needs to look outside the community. The strategy of hooking contractors into a local supply chain is particularly clear in the Sheffield City Council case study. The contracts are with five large organisations, and the Council seeks to connect them to local social enterprises.

Market gaps

For many of the case studies, momentum was easiest to find where there was an observed market gap. Public bodies are more willing to experiment in those areas because they have something to gain in the form of reduced costs. This is how Gloucestershire County Council started work with foster care, how Sheffield City Council started work with construction, and how Lincolnshire County Council started work with youth education. In the cases of Liverpool City Council and London Borough of Ealing, there was no market until the Councils developed one by using social enterprises to deliver services.

Start big

Sometimes big headline campaigns are easier to push forward than small changes. Many of the case studies were part of a large city- or countywide effort, rather than the work of one or two people plugging away. The work in Sheffield, Merseyside, and Cornwall is an example of a larger commitment upfront.

New consortium or group

Cornwall Food Programme, Fusion 21, and the Sheffield Homes consortium are all examples of new consortia or groups formed to head up a major effort in procurement. The trick in these cases is the political will from the top.

Policy document

As useless as policy documents may often seem, they can set the tone for a new initiative or approach, especially if followed through with specific actions. For instance, Doncaster Metropolitan Borough Council produced a 'zero-waste strategy'. The mayor issued the document, and there are people in place at the Council to deliver the strategy.

Rural issues

A lot of the work **nef** has undertaken in the last five years, particularly around procurement, has generated some important points for regional variation in approach. The good thing is that the philosophy is the same: If you are committed to getting more for your money, you will find a way. The issues raised below are worth considering no matter where the public body is based but are particularly poignant if in a rural area.

Dispersal of population and suppliers

The overwhelming difference between rural and other areas is that rural areas have a far greater dispersal of both residential and business populations. There are two implications of this dispersal:

First, finding solutions entails thinking at a larger geographical level. Public bodies often need to look at the county as a whole, such as with Northumberland County Council or Gloucestershire County Council. If the rural area is near an urban area, such as a market town, then public bodies have to look at the urban area as well since people often commute between the two, such as with Lincolnshire County Council.

Second, identifying resources can be tough. Urban areas tend to have established networks of suppliers, promoted by proximity as well as good transport infrastructure. The dispersal and poorer transport infrastructure in rural areas means that viable local resources may go unnoticed without active searching.

Lincolnshire County Council set up a relationship with Hill Holt Wood by literally driving around the area looking for alternative education venues. Northumberland County Council made a lot of telephone calls and site visits to develop relationships with regional suppliers.

Need for partnership

Since the population is quite dispersed and action is required at a wider geographic level, there are more players involved. While partnership across organisations is always desirable, it is more imperative in rural areas because, at the very least, county councils will need to work with district councils.

Farming versus other activities

Food is usually the first spending category identified for changing spending behaviour, simply because we all eat every day. In rural areas, however, public bodies look at food first because of the relationship to the agricultural sector in the area. When trying to kick off action, all of the public bodies in the case studies have started where there is some momentum already. Start with food if there is energy around that issue, but as the case studies demonstrate, rural areas possess a number of assets beyond agriculture that should be explored as well. After all, food is only a small fraction of a public body's total spending.

Change starts with you

Whether you are reading this publication as a procurement professional, a social entrepreneur, a policy-maker, or simply as a concerned resident, the case studies demonstrate that there is a role for everyone. Many people affect how contracts for public goods and services are developed, authorised, and delivered. The pressure may come from those working in regeneration, in finance, in a community group, or as the chief executive of the local authority. The first step may simply be to have lunch with the person you think needs to hear this information and take it from there.

Recommendations

Key points
- Question, measure, and improve the local economic impact of public spending.

- Actively promote collaboration within and across public bodies and with local suppliers.

- Redefine costings for contracts, redefine efficiency, and join budgets with other public bodies.

- Change contracting procedure to open the playing field to as many suppliers as possible.

- Remove the layers of jargon and policy that stop passionate individuals from taking action now.

The aim of this publication is to challenge current thinking on the role of public spending, particularly procurement, and to demonstrate how the public sector could do things differently. Part 2 presents case studies representing a panoply of strategies and services the public sector delivers. Based on the lessons learned and the evidence from the case studies, let's return to the ground rules to sum up the course ahead.

Rule #1: Evidence not rhetoric

The evidence from the case studies proves that the public sector…

Can:

- Promote local economic development through public procurement.

- Develop solutions to local problems that are competitive or cost less than the alternatives.

- Deliver high quality services for the same or less money.

Must:

- Question what it is trying to buy.

- Evaluate how its spending is impacting on local regeneration objectives.

- Take action to improve the economic impact of its spending.

Rule #2: Realistic

The evidence from the case studies proves that the public sector…

Can:

- Achieve multiple objectives through public spending with current budgets, timescales, and delivery targets.

- Develop solutions to local problems using personal know-how and 'elbow grease', not having to rely constantly on 'experts' to make it happen.

- Achieve multiple objectives by working across a huge range of services types, including seemingly banal services like premises cleaning.

Must:

- Give staff the space and time to develop synergies and find creative ways to achieve multiple objectives using the same amount of money.

- Consider every aspect of spending as an opportunity for improvement.

- Seek out businesses, both inside and outside the local economy, that can help innovate in achieving regeneration through procurement.

Rule #3: Money-focused

The evidence from the case studies proves that the public sector…

Can:

- Deliver the same or better quality services for the same or less money than they are already spending.

- Save money by working collaboratively with suppliers to develop solutions to local problems.

- Achieve savings across budgets by developing solutions that achieve multiple objectives.

Must:

- Redefine how it costs out and structures public contracts to consider the wider impacts of the goods and services it purchases.

- Rethink what it means by efficiency to consider the impacts of purchasing on other aspects of public budgets in both the short and long terms.

- Join up different public bodies in the same geographic areas to consider how they can use their collective purchasing power more creatively.

Rule #4: Legal

The evidence from the case studies proves that the public sector…

Can:

- Legally promote creative solutions to local problems.

- Legally develop local capacity and a healthy local economy through public spending.

- Legally foster enterprise development through public spending.

Must:

- Proactively foster the participation of SMEs in competing for contracts in order to attain a more competitive and better quality service.

- Pursue open accounting practices where possible to deliver services that are more effective and for the same or less money.

- Incorporate social benefits into contracting in order to achieve strategic aims and to account for the full costs of delivering public services.

Rule #5: Understandable

The evidence from the case studies proves that the public sector…

Can:

- Take action swiftly and with immediate results.

- Promote regeneration through even very simple actions.

- Inspire communities and regions to take action.

Must:

- Promote and reward innovation to achieve multiple objectives, even where there is a risk of failure.

- Work with enterprises in the community to inform and improve the way it delivers public services.

- Dispense with jargon and challenge colleagues to identify what they are really trying to achieve.

Change is possible. If you work in the public sector, then you see how you can take action now to buy what matters. If you work outside the public sector, you can use this publication to rally support for more creative approaches to public spending.

This publication challenges orthodox thinking on the role of public spending and shows how better ways of procuring goods and services can create better places to live for everybody. If each person reading now takes away one idea for action, then the potential collective impact will be massive.

Part 2: Walking the walk

"We've just been audited, and they did find that this new contract [with local social enterprise, Bulky Bob's] is working out cheaper than the previous one!"

David Hodnett, Liverpool City Council

"The target cost for all materials was about £158,000. But owing to our collaboration with the supply chain and the installer, the actual price we paid for the materials equated to £112,000. That's a savings of £46,000 for just one contract."

Mark Burnett, Riverside Housing Association

"... we've seen signs of a reduction in vandalism and reported crime since the social enterprises are getting the hard-to-reach into jobs."

Janet Sharpe, Sheffield Homes

"Furthermore, the young people who have experienced Hill Holt Wood have generally stayed out of the offending and anti-social cycle. They have gone on to contribute positively towards society with the skills they have obtained and become an asset, rather than a drain on their local communities."

Nigel Key, Lincolnshire Policy Authority

"The other tenders had strengths but did not stretch or innovate to the extent required by Ealing at a time of root and branch organisational change. ECT best demonstrated understanding of the integrated nature of the contract, which is not the traditional set of separates but is led by recycling and waste; ECT understands waste minimisation, which is what 60 per cent of the contract is really about."

Earl McKenzie, London Borough of Ealing

"It has stimulated thinking on regeneration activity and how this relates to procurement and the two can go further to proactively involve local and small suppliers without breaking EC legislation."

Barry Mitchell, Northumberland County Council

"As we get companies on board, we develop better relationships, and these new ideas come up out of the work we're already doing."

Nathan Harrow, Cornwall Food Programme

Case studies overview

Service area	Cut costs while promoting economic development by...
Food	**Finding local suppliers that can tailor their product to local needs**
St Peter's Primary School	Invests half of food budget back into local economy
	Generated a 40 per cent increase in meal uptake due to higher quality
	Hired one additional staff person to deliver increased uptake
Northumberland County Council	Invests half of regional food contract back into local economy
	Connected with new, local suppliers for fresh products such as bread
Cornwall Food Programme	Invests over £100,000 on food spending back into local economy
	Saves money on local high-quality cheese
	Sources more nutritious ice cream that patients actually eat
Lothian PCT	Invests £40,000 of spending on sandwiches back into the local economy
	Maintained seamless supply of sandwiches despite organisational changes
	Promotes social inclusion of people with severe mental health problems at no extra cost
Construction	**Developing local skills and supplier capacity to meet market demand**
Sheffield City Council	Invests 20 per cent of construction spending back into the most disadvantaged neighbourhoods in the local economy
	Reduced vandalism and crime
	Reduced future costs by developing skilled pool of local labour
Riverside Housing Association	Created 194 full-time jobs
	Saved £46,000 on a central heating refurbishment contract

Public spending for public benefit

Service area	Cut costs while promoting regeneration by...
Waste minimisation	**Working with businesses that can provide an integrated solution**
Liverpool City Council	Saves over £15,000 in landfill costs
	Meets twice as many pick-up calls for less money
	Promotes social inclusion of people from disadvantaged areas at no extra cost
London Borough of Ealing	Invests over £2 million back into the local economy
	Retained customers and reduced customer complaints
	Delivers community transport at no extra cost
Youth services	**Investing strategically so services pay off as young people mature**
Lincolnshire County Council	Reduced anti-social behaviour
	Develops growing pool of local skills to maintain and grow local economy in the future
	Saves over £70,000 per year on external placement
Gloucestershire County Council	Saved money on placements
	Developed competitive business that now services councils across the UK
Back office services	**Delivering the most mundane of jobs using local resources**
University of Wales Institute Cardiff	Invests over half of spending on car hire back into the local economy
	Reduced prices for car hire spending across Wales
Reading Borough Council	Invests spending on cleaning services back into the local economy
	Promotes social inclusion of people with learning disabilities at no extra cost

Public spending for public benefit

Food

Key points:

- Finding high quality, competitively priced food is feasible in schools, hospitals, and local authorities.

- Local suppliers were able to deliver food that was healthier and cheaper than the national alternatives.

- Local suppliers were able to help the public body find ways to deliver additional food items (beyond those initially requested) in innovative ways that also saved the public body money.

- There are direct, but less quantified, impacts on health, particularly for hospital patients and schoolchildren.

Food, glorious food! Food hits the top of everyone's list when it comes to discussions of public spending, health, economics, and rural livelihoods.

St Peter's Church of England Primary School

Approach
The catering manager at a primary school knew there must be a way to get better quality food into her school. So she simply put foot to pavement to find local alternatives. Five years on, over half of the school menu is sourced from local business for the same or less money than before, and student uptake of meals has increased by 40 per cent.

Service supplied
Provision of meat, eggs, milk, and vegetables from local businesses for school meals.

Background

Jeanette Orrey is the catering manager at St Peter's in East Bridgford, Nottinghamshire, and has been there for 14 years. Like many people in her position, Jeanette noticed that children were selecting unhealthy food at mealtimes. She noted, however, that this wasn't simply because of taste. There was a lack of education in the school about food: where it comes from, how it's produced, and how food impacts on health.

This overall concern was paired with a very practical concern in the workplace about stability. School kitchen staff frequently work ad hoc, not on a fixed contract. This means that anyone working in a school kitchen is at risk of working variable hours from week to week based on how many meals students elect to eat at the school. "The way we were working before, if we lost five dinners, then the following week the ladies' hours would be cut by 15 minutes." Working on such a schedule not only created an insecure work situation for employees but also alienated the kitchen staff from the rest of the school.

Action

Jeanette knew there must be some viable local alternatives, so she started talking to local suppliers. "Meat was a priority," Jeanette explains, "so I literally got in the car and went round to the farm shops and asked if they were interested." It was possible to agree a competitive price for the meat because Jeanette could offer a 38-week contract. "The farmers already had a market for the more expensive cuts, so this was a good way for them to sell off their cheaper meat. It was worth the risk for them since it was a long-term contract."

Jeanette took the same approach with milk, eggs, and vegetables. Each time, the suppliers greeted Jeannette's story of getting more local food into the school with support. As with the meat supplier, these other suppliers were able to supply St Peter's at a competitive price in exchange for the long-term contract.

Legality

This approach highlights a common misconception about public procurement: you don't have to go through an extensive EU-wide search for every single purchase. Public bodies in the UK must advertise contracts EU-wide if they are over £154,477. In the case of St Peter's, as with many public bodies, the majority of its spending falls below this threshold. Public bodies still need to demonstrate they've searched for a competitive supplier for spending below the EU threshold. Since the new suppliers came in at the same or lower price as the current suppliers, this was straightforward.

To find alternative suppliers for smaller food contracts, Jeanette reviewed the last Environmental Health Officer's (EHO) report and confirmed registration with the local authority. Jeanette also carries an audit trail for herself and each supplier.

Economic impact

Since starting this transformation in school food at St Peter's, school meal uptake has increased by *40 per cent*. Now, 85 per cent of all students are buying school meals. St Peter's charges a price that is not far above at-cost, but the increased uptake means a little more money for the school to re-invest.

One way St Peter's re-invested the extra income was to buy a 'rumbler and slicer', a piece of equipment that cleans potatoes and root vegetables like carrots. Jeanette reckons the rumbler paid for itself in 20 weeks because St Peter's was then able to buy potatoes and carrots for less money than it was paying the previous supplier. The school previously bought pre-peeled and packaged potatoes and carrots. The school now buys these items in a sack and prepares them in-house. In addition to reducing costs and packaging waste, Jeanette notes another improvement: "This kind of work also gave self-respect back to those working in the kitchen; people knew they were actually achieving something."

The increased meal uptake has also generated employment. Jeanette explains, "I haven't had to cut hours in the last five years. In fact, we've taken on one staff person!" Due to the increased morale in the kitchen, Jeanette also notes, "We've retained staff as well."

Of St Peter's total food budget of roughly £23,000, the school now spends *half* of it with local suppliers. Jeanette hasn't completed a full LM3 for St Peter's, but whenever she explains the multiplier effect, people's eyes light up. "Now that I present all over the country, when I do those presentations about the local economy, those figures make people stop and think," Jeanette comments. "People come up to me and say they simply hadn't thought about it before."

The work at St Peter's has motivated other organisations in the community to follow suit. For instance, the local post office now uses the same local milk supplier as St Peter's, and parents use the same local farm shop to buy local meat.

Additional impacts

St Peter's has turned food into yet another facet of education. While the financial value of Jeanette's work has enabled her to build momentum within the school, Jeanette notes a number of important social changes.

First, these local suppliers have become another educational resource for the school. St Peter's, for instance, uses the farm shops as a place to take the children to learn about healthy eating, which is a part of all school curricula now.

Second, the work at St Peter's has raised awareness about food culture, particularly the social value of food. Jeanette notes, "When I present, not only do people begin to think about the local economy, but they also begin to see food shopping as a social experience, which they didn't before."

Finally, while Jeanette doesn't have statistics to prove that all children at St Peter's are healthier and smarter now, she does reflect on one instance that represents daily life for her, "I went into a local café for a coffee, and it turned out that one of my pupils was there. She's sitting in front of a jacket potato with tuna and salad, and I as I walk in, her mum tells me, 'She chose this herself!' Mind you, the girl is five years old."

Next steps

Jeanette's success at St Peter's earned her national media attention and a role at the Soil Association as a policy advisor on school food purchasing. Jeanette still works at St Peter's, but she now spends much of her time supporting other schools in setting up similar ventures. All the schools Jeanette has worked with, both urban and rural, have seen success. Jeanette hopes to work with local authorities directly so that schools do not have to opt out of their county council catering relationship to source local food, but rather to have schools and local authorities working together. The next case study on Northumberland County Council shows how this is possible.

Northumberland County Council

Approach
A county council decided to measure and improve its local economic impact, and it used food supply contracts as an opportunity to test the measuring methodology and focus energy. The investment yielded improved relations with local suppliers, a more responsive regional business support network, and more competitive and localised sourcing of food for the food supply contract.

Service supplied
Provision of food supplies (including meat, milk, bread, and fruit and vegetables) for school meals, social services, residential and day care establishments, and civic catering.

Background
In January 2004, Northumberland County Council created a full-time post to evaluate the economic impact of its £245 million procurement budget and to lead efforts to maximise that impact. Barry Mitchell was brought in to do the job, which started with a benchmarking of the Council's current impact.

The process, using LM3 to measure a sampling of its spending, opened eyes across the Council. The benchmarking process found that local suppliers respent on average 76 per cent of their contracts with local people and businesses, while suppliers based outside the county respent on average 36 per cent of their contracts locally. The combination of all suppliers produced an LM3 score of 2.19, which the Council now uses as its benchmark for measuring progress. This score of 2.19 represents the averaging of the LM3 for local suppliers, 2.76, and the LM3 for non-local suppliers, 1.36. What Barry found when he looked more closely at these figures was that if the Council found ways to shift 10 per cent of its current spending on non-local suppliers to local suppliers, this would generate an additional £34 million for the local economy.

In spring of that year, the Council's food supply contracts, for which it contracts for food on behalf of all schools and care facilities in Northumberland, came up for renewal. The Council decided to use this annual £3 million opportunity to make some changes.

Action

The first step was to reach out to the businesses and support organisations in the area. "We organised a seminar aimed at communicating the contract needs to all the small and local food suppliers, together with those food and transport suppliers already supplying the Council," explains Barry. "We went through the food tender process and also encouraged a lot of the second-tier suppliers to complete the exercise to achieve approved supplier list status, even if they might not compete for and win this tender." The Council hadn't previously contracted for bread, so Barry personally contacted regional bread suppliers to alert them to the contract opportunity.

Barry recognised that some of the businesses might need business and technical assistance, so the second step was to get the regional Business Link and local umbrella organisation, Northumbria Larder, on board. "It was great to be able to match up businesses with business support organisations and to build trust between the two groups," explains Barry. "We later found out that a number of businesses went to Business Link and Northumbria Larder and were provided with advice and help including business and technical assistance in order to put tenders together and complete the required tender documentation."

The third step was to alter the specifications in the upcoming tender to open up the playing field to all types of businesses. "We split the contract into lots," explains Barry, "allowing businesses to bid on a combination of up to seven food categories in four geographic areas of the county." This system in fact gave Northumberland County Council the most competitive total service because it could combine tenders in a number of ways. The procurement team also used Best Value criteria, weighting quality and price at a ratio of 60:40. The quality criteria also required that the contractor be prepared to assist the Council's Catering Services Department in pursuing a sustainable food procurement strategy.

Legality

The arrangements for the purchase of goods and services by the Council are governed by EU Procurement Directives, UK legislation, and the Council's own finance and contract rules underpinned by the corporate procurement strategy. The directives and regulations require local authorities to follow detailed procedures for all purchases above financial thresholds, and they are reviewed every two years. The current threshold is £154,477 for supplies and services and £3.8 million for works. Since the food contract had a total value of approximately £3 million per annum, it fell under formal EU procedure. Under this legislation, the Council needed to follow some basic principles for any contract over the threshold:

- Place a tender notice in the supplement to the Official Journal of the European Union (OJEU) to give all potential suppliers in the EU an equal opportunity to tender.

- Invite tenders in accordance with one of the prescribed procedures (open, restricted, negotiated). Each procedure imposes minimum timescales covering the tender activities to ensure that reasonable time to respond to adverts and prepare submissions is given to interested parties.

- Place a notice of contract award in the OJEU. Unsuccessful contractors must be debriefed if requested.

Breaking a contract into separate lots is an acceptable legal procedure as long as it can be justified for economic reasons rather than to circumvent thresholds. There is more administrative work involved, though the Council deemed the additional time investment to be offset by the quantity and quality of the tenders received. By breaking the contract into lots, the Council was able to select the most competitive group of tenders, securing the best price and quality for all regions within the county. While councils are not allowed to discuss particulars of a contract with any suppliers (beyond what is in the tender documentation), they are allowed to work with suppliers to make them generally more competitive.

Economic impact

"The effect of increasing awareness of the Council food tender process and encouraging local and small suppliers was evident in both the expressions of interest made and also the tenders received," notes Barry. "We saw a five-fold increase in local supplier expressions of interest."

The result of the food contract tendering process was that four of the seven product categories (meat, milk, bread, and fruit and vegetables) were awarded to local suppliers. As Barry explains, "This is a significant change for the Council as the food supply contracts were previously let on a block basis to a few large

**The ripple effect in Northumberland.
One small action has spurred activity in other sectors and other councils**

- Council budget
- Make changes to food contract
- Measure impact of budget
- Change council policy
- Re-design contract & tendering procedures
- Find ways to improve economic impact of property maintenance, sandwiches, & grass cutting contracts
- Interest from private sector
- Support private & voluntary sector
- Work with Northumberland Cheese & Lindisfarn Mead
- Work with voluntary organisations to measure & improve impact
- Change corporate procurement policy
- Set finance target to shift 10% of spending to local suppliers

Public spending for public benefit

suppliers." Barry adds, "A few of these suppliers were already supplying the Council, but in this day and age just keeping those suppliers involved is also a challenge when we face pressure to award one giant contract to one supplier instead."

In financial terms, this means that almost half of the £3 million annual contract will go to local suppliers and circulate in the local economy.

Additional impacts

The small but concrete successes of the LM3 benchmarking and the work around the regional food contract have spurred more extensive interest. "It has stimulated thinking on regeneration activity," explains Barry, "and how this relates to procurement and the two can go further to proactively involve local and small suppliers without breaking EC legislation." The new procurement strategy solidly reflects the importance of SMEs to the community's well-being, and the Council has improved its website with specific support for SMEs.

"The work on the food contract also increased the effectiveness of our links to business support organisations, such as Business Link and Northumbria Larder," notes Barry, "and it's increased the profile of the Council with local businesses, who have appreciated the efforts made to increase their opportunities for doing business." In a recent meeting with local food producers, Barry noted, "When we first met with the suppliers, they were openly hostile because they felt the Council had ignored them for a long time, but there is a real spirit of co-operation now that they feel the Council actually values the work they do."

The work of the Council has also prompted regional businesses to take action beyond the public spending sphere. "A few local producers have been encouraged to attain EU protected name status," explains Barry, "and a local cheese producer currently has a full application submitted to Defra for consideration, with pending applications for a fish supplier and another for mead." Attaining EU protected name status could lead to a potential marketing advantage for suppliers and a profile boost for Northumberland.

Next steps

The benchmarking work that Northumberland County Council performed has sparked the interest of others in the area. Barry notes, "There has been interest by the private sector in the work we're doing, and work has been jointly ongoing with a large global private sector company. The parent office had required their plant sites to establish their annual worth to the local community, and we've adapted the LM3 methodology that we used to benchmark our own economic impact to do this."

The Council plans to continue funding Barry to develop and expand his work. Barry reviews some of the top items for next year, "We have further presentations to encourage awareness; the Director of the Regional Centre of Excellence has requested a specific presentation along with district council representatives; we will continue to liaise with Business Link representatives on tender opportunities and assist the current selected EU protected name applicants along with some new applications; and we'll continue to work with food suppliers to streamline approved supplier list applications. We will also apply the LM3 methodology in forthcoming tenders in areas ranging from property construction, verge cutting, and public transport provision."

The finance department has since officially set a target of shifting ten per cent of procurement spending to local sources within the next three years.

Cornwall Food Programme, operated by the Cornwall Healthcare Community

Approach
A consortium of NHS Trusts in Cornwall decided to tap into the thriving agricultural sector of the region in an effort to get top-quality food to hospital patients while also adding value to the economy. In a little over one year, hospitals are already serving local cheese and ice cream, and fresh fish is on the way.

Service supplied
Ice cream and cheese.

Background
Cornwall Healthcare Community (CHC) is a consortium of the five NHS Trusts in Cornwall. A series of changes in 1999 led CHC to rethink how it supplied food to its hospitals. After successfully developing in-house capacity to produce cook-freeze meals for the Maternity Unit at Royal Cornwall Hospital, managers began to ask: "If we can do this for one hospital, why not for the whole county?"

Cornwall Healthcare Community subsequently developed the Cornwall Food Programme (CFP) in 2003 to address the food supply needs of health services in Cornwall while also addressing the economic concerns of the area, one of the most disadvantaged areas in the UK.

Action 1: Ice cream
The first action the CFP took may appear somewhat surprising on face value: They changed ice cream suppliers. Nathan Harrow and Roy Heath, managers of

the CFP, explain, "After doing the rounds of a 900-bed facility, the ice cream on patients' plates would be melted. This was due to the fact that the previous supplier pumped a lot of air into the cream to reduce costs, along with using mediocre ingredients." Nathan and Roy felt this was a waste of resources, and that there must be a local solution in a county renowned for its dairy products.

The first discussion with local suppliers generated much goodwill but no competitive ice cream suppliers, so CFP engaged further with willing suppliers. Callestick Farm is a large business but has longstanding local roots, an on-site herd of cows, and was open to discussion with CFP. Together, they identified ways to lower Callestick's prices without compromising quality.

The first step was to change the portion size. Callestick used a larger portion size than needed by CFP, which would be wasted on patients with smaller appetites anyway. The second step was to strip away the flashy packaging since CFP had a captive audience. Finally, CFP noted that Callestick's ice cream contained more nutritional value than that of the national supplier. "While you may wonder, 'what nutrition is there in ice cream?!'", muses Nathan, "getting any nutrition into short-stay patients is a priority, and ice cream has plenty of calcium, protein, and vitamins A and D." In fact, Callestick's ice cream had 50 per cent more protein than the previous supplier's. CFP altered the specifications of its ice cream contract to require a higher nutritional value. On the basis of the revised specifications, the national contractors declined to even submit bids, and Callestick won the contract on both price and quality.

Legality

This approach challenges the assumptions many procurement officers make; namely, you *are* able to craft a contract that opens up the playing field to local and small enterprises by rethinking the requirements of the contract. CFP played ball by holding a meeting in advance of tendering to discuss the contract. No national suppliers attended because CFP was a drop in the bucket for them. CFP then crafted a contract that opened up the playing field, but this is entirely legal because it was based on nutritional requirements, not locality. CFP then advertised this contract nationally (since it was under £100,000), enabling any business to bid. Again, national suppliers could have bid for the contract, but their nutritional requirements are lower, so they chose not to.

Action 2: Cheese

The second action CFP took was to identify a suitable local cheese supplier. Similar to the work with Callestick Farm, CFP knew there were top-quality cheese producers in the county, just that they were supplying to national markets and not Cornwall.

Nathan and Roy met with Cornish Country Larder and found an immediate win-win situation. Cornish Country Larder produces cheese primarily for supermarkets, which have very tight specifications for size, colour, etc. Anything that is outside these parameters is considered 'off-spec'. The supplier usually has no choice but to send off-spec products to a processor at a very low price. The agreement reached between CFP and Cornish Country Larder is simple. If CFP needs cheese, they can go to Cornish Country Larder to get it.

Economic impact

The sourcing of local ice cream has helped redirect almost £100,000 (the value of the contract) back into the Cornwall economy for a superior product. Most importantly, patients are happier. One elderly patient's husband later came to the hospital to find out the brand of ice cream served in the hospital because it was the only thing his wife would eat. Patients have noticed a difference, and this has been reflected in patient feedback, such as this comment: "Food presented is very high quality and most enjoyable. The patients and people of Cornwall will benefit greatly when the Food Production Unit is a reality. Thank you for this opportunity of 'tasting the future'!"

This story of local cheese is also good for everyone. CFP actually pays *less* for this cheese than it was paying through a national supplier. Cornish Country Larder makes *more* from the sale than sending it to the processor; and hospital patients are in for a treat when they get their cheese and biscuits!

In addition to the work on ice cream and cheese, CFP has taken a number of steps to improve its local economic impact. Jenny Thatcher, a then-master's student looking at various forms of economic evaluation, used LM3 to evaluate the CFP's overall impact and found a score range of 1.81 to 1.95, varying in score based on how results from suppliers and staff were treated. When Jenny looked only at how CFP respent its money, called LM2, the score came to 1.52. These numbers are made more meaningful when compared with the food-sourcing alternative employed by the Cornwall Partnership Trust (CPT). The CPT manages mental healthcare facilities in Cornwall and contracts with Tillery Valley, a national contractor based in Wales. Jenny looked at how CPT spent its money (LM2), and calculated a score of 1.05. This means that if you compare the LM2 score for the Cornwall Food Programme (1.52) versus the LM2 score for the CPT (1.05), every £100,000 spent by the Cornwall Food Programme generates £47,000 more for the Cornwall economy.[35]

---

35 Jenny Thatcher's full report is available at the following website:
www.brad.ac.uk/acad/envsci/infostore/cornwall/foodprgramme.pdf

Additional impacts

CFP's approach has generated not only direct economic benefits to Cornwall but additional benefits for the county as well.

The most important added benefit is the snowball effect of working with open-minded companies (whether they are local or otherwise). "As we get companies on board," Roy explains, "we develop better relationships, and these new ideas come up out of the work we're already doing." For instance, the owner of Cornish Country Larder alerted Nathan and Roy to the fact that a major by-product of cheese production is whey butter, which can be used in place of regular butter. Chefs in the Cornwall Healthcare Community are now trialling whey butter in pastries. If patient response is positive, then CFP will have identified a cheap alternative to butter that also happens to reduce waste and transport.

CFP and Cornish Country Larder have also made strides with grated cheese. CFP currently buys 1,000-kilo blocks of cheddar cheese that they grate in-house using an employee already doing other work. Instead, Cornish Country Larder offered to grate cheddar off-cuts, which reduces CFP's packaging, equipment, and salary costs.

Nathan and Roy also note a feeling of reciprocity with local businesses that does not exist with national companies. Nathan and Roy recall, "There was this time when one of our vans broke down, and we needed a refrigerated van for a few weeks. One of the local companies let us borrow one of his. Try getting a national company to do that!"

Next steps

CFP is ploughing forward with more changes. Next on the horizon is fresh fish. Few people expected CFP to find a way to source fresh fish in hospitals. In fact, the NHS doesn't even have a national framework agreement in place for fresh fish. As with ice cream and cheese, CFP is in the midst of securing a competitive contract with a local fish and fish cake supplier simply through holding open discussions with him. The process works to everyone's benefit because the fish supplier has found a new buyer, and CFP has found a fish supplier who is actually *cheaper* than its current supplier! "With the national supplier," Roy explains, "we had fish of bizarre sizes and dubious quality, but we are able to specify 100 gram portions with this local guy."

CFP is also taking this message out to hospital staff by offering access to a fruit-and-vegetable-box scheme. CFP found a local supplier simply by going out and talking with people. "We found this supplier called Newquay Fruit and Veg and asked him why he wasn't trying to supply to us previously," Nathan and Roy explain, "and he said that he didn't know the process, and that no one had sought out the local market." CFP is now connecting Newquay Fruit and Veg to other local suppliers so that they can supply into the box scheme.

Lothian Primary Care Trust/Royal Edinburgh Hospital food services

The role of health-related institutions is to promote good health. It makes a lot of sense, therefore, that the NHS should promote health not only among patients but also through its purchasing decisions. That is what Lothian Primary Care Trust (PCT) has done for many years through one of its services providers, Rolls on Wheels.

The Lothian PCT is comprised of a number of health-related institutions, including the Royal Edinburgh Hospital, which is the largest mental health hospital in the Lothians. In 1999, the PCT shut down Gogarburn Hospital, which had previously supplied lunches to smaller day hospitals in the PCT. These hospitals, including Royal Edinburgh Hospital, became stretched to capacity after the closure.

The Royal Edinburgh Hospital needed to find an alternative source for lunches after the Gogarburn closure, so it approached Rolls on Wheels, one of the PCT's approved suppliers. Rolls on Wheels, a social firm based in Edinburgh, had previously supplied Gogarburn Hospital with filled rolls. James Belton, Business Development Manager at Rolls on Wheels, explains, "After a number of meetings, it was agreed that Rolls on Wheels would supply the hospital for 12 months, and we've continued to supply this service for the past five years."

The relationship has proven beneficial to both Rolls on Wheels and the PCT. At a time of great transition, the Royal Edinburgh Hospital was able to maintain service delivery without diverting resources from its core workload. The hospital also saved money because it avoided having to employ another driver or provide the necessary delivery vehicle just for an hour and a half's worth of activity a day. For Rolls on Wheels, the new work expanded its client portfolio and enabled it to cover part of the cost of a new vehicle that could serve multiple clients as well as creating employment opportunities.

The manner in which Rolls on Wheels operates enables the PCT to promote health, social inclusion, and regeneration for no extra cost. As a social firm, Rolls on Wheels seeks to bring people with severe and enduring mental health problems into meaningful employment. This fits precisely with the PCT's agenda, and particularly with Royal Edinburgh Hospital. Rolls on Wheels also re-invests its profits back into employment creation and into community development areas in disadvantaged areas of Edinburgh.

Rolls on Wheels carried out an LM3 evaluation and found a score of 1.99. This means that every £100 that the PCT spends with Rolls on Wheels generates an additional £99 for the local economy, on top of promoting social inclusion that carries savings with it as well. With a total current turnover of £185,000 per year, this represents a significant re-investment in Edinburgh. "The consistent work with the PCT has helped Rolls on Wheels stabilise and grow as a business," explains James. "Turnover has increased five fold since 1997, and the company now employs seven staff and provides places for 28 trainees." Meanwhile, the contract with the Royal Edinburgh Hospital currently comprises about 11 per cent of Rolls on Wheels' turnover, which means Rolls on Wheels is not dependent on the hospital for succeeding as a business.

Construction

Key points

- Developing local solutions is essential to delivering construction projects because demand outstrips supply, even at the national level.

- Local authorities and housing associations can use construction programmes to skill up local people in professions that will remain in high demand.

- Developing local solutions saves money, particularly through better supply chain management and partnership with the supply chain delivering construction work.

The metaphor is just too obvious to avoid here: construction is not simply about putting up buildings but about laying the foundations for healthy communities that will last for years. Construction is also one sector in which the demand for construction work far outstrips the labour supply. This imbalance has caused construction prices to go through the roof and often results in massive delays. For these reasons, attempts to build local capacity will pay off in terms of bringing down construction costs and timeframes.

Sheffield City Council/Sheffield Homes

Approach
Using an arms-length management organisation, a local council is working with major construction companies and social enterprises to rebuild the local economy along with the housing stock.

Service supplied
Housing refurbishment and development.

Background

Since 1997, councils across the UK were given funding and targets to implement the national Decent Homes Programme, intended to bring all social housing up to 'decent' standards. Sheffield City Council responded to the requirements of the programme by setting up an arms-length management organisation (ALMO), Sheffield Homes, to oversee the £1 billion initiative.

But there's a twist. The Council wanted to use this massive inflow of money to create permanent economic change as part of its Closing the Gap agenda. The challenge was to create thousands of local employment and training opportunities. The Decent Homes Programme provided the opportunity to make a dramatic change in some of the city's most disadvantaged neighbourhoods. Since the timeframe for the Decent Homes Programme is tight (all homes have to be improved by 2010), the Council reckoned it needed to foster a partnership between five major national contractors to undertake the work.

"Large national companies are well placed to meet the demands of complex investment programmes because they can cope with high volumes of work and changes in workforce," explains Janet Sharpe, Investment Manager at Sheffield Homes. "These characteristics mean large companies can incorporate social enterprises into their supply chain and subcontracting arrangements to give the social enterprises financial security without giving up their own independence."

Previous experience with large contractors had left the Council with concerns. Janet recalls, "Big contractors tend to be renowned for coming in to a community where they have no relationship, winning contracts based on lowest price, and as soon as the work is done, the contractors are gone along with the employment opportunities." Janet compared this to the sense people have about smaller enterprises, "By growing social enterprises locally, for instance, it's something people really care about; they have a sense of ownership, and they often sit as directors on the board, and they have a passionate commitment to improving housing and the quality of the local environment." Janet adds, "They can demonstrate best value, and in revenue terms, vandalism and reported anti-social behaviour incidents tend to decrease."

Janet believes that social enterprises would find it difficult to compete with large companies given the pressure to deliver complex capital projects with tight timescales. "National companies are often committed to leaving a legacy after all the capital work is completed to show how they have contributed to a better local economy," explains Janet, "and working with social enterprises is a way to achieve that."

The Council found itself needing to work with larger businesses to achieve the Decent Homes Programme targets in time, but it felt the programme presented an opportunity to improve local employment rates because construction work would open up more job opportunities for local residents. The trick was to develop skilled labour and social enterprises that could competitively supply the larger businesses in carrying out the Decent Homes Programme.

Action

The Council first identified five key large construction companies to work with at a high level, which became a partnership that is managed by Sheffield Homes. "The five big companies have been really excellent about working with us because they can see the benefits for themselves," explains Janet. The catch is that the companies are all committed to delivering at least 10 per cent of their work through social enterprises, as long as Sheffield Homes develops competitive social enterprises to help deliver that work. The onus falls on Sheffield Homes to facilitate, negotiate, and develop viable supply chains, but the agreement means that the five companies will work with those supply chains as long as Sheffield Homes provides the opportunities for them to do so.

"The bottom line is that if the companies want to do work in Sheffield, they have to abide by these rules," Janet explains. Sheffield Homes, in partnership with the contracting companies, is in the midst of facilitating the development of a further three community building companies to help the principal companies deliver the Decent Homes construction work. Janet continues, "The larger companies are happy to comply because we have such an incredible shortage of trades in Sheffield, such as joinery, decoration, plumbing, and electrical trades, that the larger companies can find social enterprises to be a cheaper and more secure source of labour rather than outsourcing every time; it's in their interest." Again, the companies are not required to work with these social enterprises unless they are competitive, but in the current hot construction market, this is achievable for Sheffield Homes.

Janet offers an example of how this is already working, "For instance, Keepmoat has contributed a substantial amount of its own money and time to help establish a new locally based company to deliver some of the softer trades where it is becoming impossible to recruit, creating a long-term company that will be commercially sustainable in years to come. They then know that they have a small company that can deliver this work with a secured source of labour rather than continually tendering every time."

One of the largest social enterprises that Sheffield Homes works with is Sheffield Rebuild. "Back when Sheffield Rebuild started in 1996, we had a lot of SRB [Single Regeneration Budget] funding that we were able to use to get them up and running," explains Janet. "We had a separate revenue stream that we could use to support the cost of setting up businesses, delivering training, technical assistance, and so on. We were able to separate out those costs from the actual costs of construction work."

This means that Sheffield Rebuild was able to legitimately compete under Best Value procurement rules while the Council used SRB funding to support elements that were not considered core to the basic construction work. "Now we don't support them at all," notes Janet. "We only use our money for the construction service, and Sheffield Rebuild supports its training activity from CITB, Objective 1/ESF grants, or Sheffield's new Construction Job Match Initiative."[36]

Legality

Sheffield's approach is legal because it doesn't specify locality and abides by Best Value rules of engagement. The agreement with the key organisations is around a mode of production. The strategy the Council used in previous years to get Sheffield Rebuild up and running is completely legal because the Council used separate funds earmarked for developing enterprises and enterprise capacity.

The agreement with the large businesses to source from social enterprises is voluntary since the Council cannot make this a requirement; however, in this instance, the interests of the Council and the business converge because social enterprises can offer a competitive service in construction.

Economic impact

The strategy is already paying off. "We keep working with social enterprises because we're getting some excellent results in terms of getting people furthest from employment into employment," Janet notes, "and we're also seeing a really high quality of training and a lot of local community support because it's something the area feels ownership of – the community is fully involved in creating local businesses that they feel they have been part of setting up, so many of the employees and board members, for instance, are locally recruited."

An LM3 evaluation of one of the many contracts managed by Sheffield Homes and delivered by Sheffield Rebuild produced a score of 2.25. This means that every £100 the Council spends on housing work generates an additional £125 for the local economy. A further breakdown of this spending showed that 20 per cent of the total contract was spent in the immediate area of the construction project, which is in one of the most disadvantaged areas of Sheffield.

Janet adds, "I haven't measured this part, but I have noted that shops are staying in business because people have more disposable income in a way they didn't

---

[36] CITB stands for the Construction Industry Training Board and more information is available at www.citb.org.uk; ESF stands for European Social Fund and more information is available at www.esf.gov.uk

before." Imagine if 20 per cent of a typical £10 million construction project went straight into the pockets of local people in the form of income? This is what Sheffield is trying to make a reality.

Additional impacts

In addition to the injection of income into the city's most disadvantaged areas, the Council has noted other benefits. "At the very least, we now have a much better relationship with our tenants, residents, and local shops and businesses," Janet observes, "and we've seen signs of a reduction in vandalism and reported crime since the social enterprises are getting the hard-to-reach into jobs."

Janet feels comfortable with this observation considering that Sheffield Rebuild, which is one of several social enterprises, now employs 160 people, many of whom have come from disadvantaged communities. Many of these employees came through training on Sheffield Rebuild contracts and now work there full-time. "Sheffield Rebuild will not be able to address the majority of social problems in these areas," Janet explains, "but it is starting to help."

The shortage of labour and skills has provided a unique opportunity for Sheffield Homes. "Providing opportunities to reskill long-term unemployed people from disadvantaged areas not only reduces regional skill shortages in key trades, but it also enables people to move from claiming benefits into full-time employment and gaining recognised national qualifications that can lead to lucrative careers in construction," explains Janet, "and that income then goes into local shops and the whole economy starts to feel the benefit."

Finally, the businesses have found a cheaper and more secure labour pool, which benefits their profit margin. These market gaps provide ideal opportunities for Sheffield Homes to develop social enterprises to meet a market need competitively.

Next steps

Sheffield Homes will continue to work with the larger businesses to identify and develop competitive social enterprises to feed into the supply chain. Concurrently, Sheffield Homes will look to facilitate the development of more social enterprises that can meet market shortages in trades such as tile hanging, plumbing, building surveying, tenant liaison, translation, and community research.

Riverside Housing Association/Fusion 21

A registered social landlord (RSL) joined up with six other RSLs and the local authority to use their collective purchasing power not only to reduce costs but also to promote local jobs and businesses. All partners have enjoyed lower costs while maintaining or improving quality, and the region has seen an increase in local capacity.

Service supplied
Installation of windows, kitchens and bathrooms, and central heating systems for residential buildings.

Background
Mark Burnett, a Project Manager at Riverside Housing Association (Riverside), explains, "On top of a chronic skills shortage in the construction industry, there has been a massive upturn in construction due to the strong economy and various government initiatives like the Decent Homes Programme that requires the property owned by RSLs to achieve a certain standard by 2010." These trends have led to price inflation in the construction sector. Mark further explains, "The rising costs have led Riverside, along with its partner RSLs, to consider how they would continue to deliver the same or even more extensive asset management services under current government budgetary constraints, where income is capped."

Action

In 2002, Knowsley Metropolitan Borough Council led efforts in Merseyside to maximise the value of ever-tighter RSL budgets. The partnership formed between the Council and RSLs, known as Fusion 21, aimed to respond to the two key issues Mark cited as an issue for Riverside: 1) rising construction contract prices in the face of rent capping in the social housing sector and 2) a shortage of skills within the construction industry in Merseyside.

Before joining Fusion 21, Riverside's traditional procurement policy was to employ a sole contractor to manage and deliver all of the necessary installation as well as the supply chain delivering that installation. The Fusion 21 model now enables Riverside to manage not only the installation costs but also the product costs. "All procurement data is captured centrally," explains Mark, "which enables us to monitor and analyse costs, which in turn means that actual costs are the same, or at least very close to, predicted costs."

A key innovation of Fusion 21 is collaborative working, particularly with the suppliers, to find solutions to reducing costs while maintaining quality. The use of 'product teams' has enabled Riverside to work with its partners to find quick solutions to problems that cannot be easily resolved at project or site level. "We have product teams covering all of the key work streams, such as windows, bathrooms, and kitchens," Mark points out. Each product team represents a pooling of experience on design and installation performance. As Mark explains, "Each product team includes expert staff from Riverside, the other RSLs, the installers, the manufacturers, tenant members of the RSLs, a team manager, and a team mentor."

Mark offers the examples of the 'window product team', "There are four different suppliers of window profiles within the window workstream, but only one locking mechanism is specified, and it's supplied by a different company. There was an issue of compatibility between the window profiles and the locking mechanism, which the product team resolved. This has led to the supplier of the locking mechanism producing a new lock that is compatible with the four different window profiles."

Using the Rethinking Construction Toolkit, Riverside also works with installers to: benchmark and compare performance, achieve Investor in People accreditation, achieve ISO[37] quality accreditation, and participate in the Considerate Constructor's Scheme, which is a voluntary code of practice seeking to minimise the negative impacts of construction sites on neighbourhoods and promote safety and environmental awareness.

---

37 ISO stands for the International Organization for Standardization and more information is available at www.iso.org

"For example," Mark explains, "we have an initiative to ensure that the entire workforce employed by installers has a Construction Skills Certification Scheme Card. This is a government-backed scheme aimed at up-skilling the workforce on sites. This has meant in some cases arranging for on-site assessments for the workforce, and we've arranged for the successful assessment of 55 on-site personnel to date." This approach allows Riverside to work with suppliers, wherever they come from, to up-skill their workforce, which is often from the local area.

Legality

The Fusion 21 model and Riverside's work dispels a widespread misconception in the public sector that public bodies cannot work collaboratively with suppliers. The key distinction is between collaboration before tendering (referred to as collusion), versus collaboration after awarding a contract, which is completely legal. "For Riverside as well as our partners," explains Mark, "the selection process had to be robust and legal, but more importantly, it had to produce a group of contractors that we felt shared our partnering ideals and had similar visions and values." Selecting suppliers for Riverside and the other partners in Fusion 21 took a little over six months.

The major steps in the process included:

- Procurement strategy agreement (while options included official OJEC advertisement (now OJEU), open invitation, select list, and direct negotiation, Fusion 21 decided to go with OJEC and place an OJEC advertisement).

- Pre-qualification questionnaire (asks in-depth questions about finances, partnering experience, quality management, health and safety, personnel and training, equality and diversity, environmental policy, and references).

- Selection process (briefing session, interview, site and office visits, target costing, and preferred partner selection).

Economic impact

Above all, despite rapidly increasing tender-price inflation and a capped income stream, Riverside has been able to provide a maintenance service to the desired number of properties by effectively managing its installation costs. "Take this central heating replacement scheme for 124 properties in the Kensington area of Liverpool for example," offers Mark. "The target cost for all materials was about £158,000. But owing to our collaboration with the supply chain and the installer, the actual price we paid for the materials equated to £112,000." That's a savings of £46,000 for just one contract. This was achieved by the direct strategic sourcing of materials from suppliers.

Also because of the 'closed loop', the installer call-off (on-site ordering) of equipment for each property within the contract can be closely scrutinised by Riverside to ensure that the actual on-site order does not vary from the proposed purchase order for each particular property (generated at survey stage) owing to unauthorised call-offs for whatever reason. In a nutshell, all material transactions are transparent, and you only pay for what is actually installed within your property.

Additional impacts

The money Riverside saves is then available to be re-invested into its properties. Riverside also invests some of this money into Fusion 21 Skills and Ambition, a construction training programme. This programme trains eligible participants in a range of construction professions, including window fitting, roofing, plastering, plumbing, kitchen/bathroom fitting, gas fitting, painting and decorating, tiling and building maintenance. The programme has trained 317 recruits since 2002, with impressive (and in fact UK record-breaking) results. The programme has led to the creation of 194 full-time jobs, and 39 clients either in training at present or on a waiting list for a job.

Next steps

Riverside and its partners will continue to identify how the Fusion 21 model can be adapted for use across other areas of operations, such as new-build developments, gas servicing, cyclical painting, and disabled adaptations. The success of the programme has attracted the attention of the Office of the Deputy Prime Minister, which wants to establish 40 new groups across the UK.

Waste minimisation

Key points
- Promoting waste minimisation saves the public sector money in both the short-term and the long-term.

- Local suppliers were able to deliver contracts that were cheaper and higher quality than their national and international counterparts.

- Local suppliers were able to boost recycling and reduce waste production for no extra cost.

- Local authorities were able to work in partnership with local suppliers to achieve long-term changes to waste rather than short-term fixes to the problem.

If you could save money by reducing waste, would you? What if you could also promote local employment opportunities and support new markets, too? Right, you would. Waste minimisation has moved from the realm of the optional to the required over the last few years. Whether or not you subscribe to the environmental philosophy behind waste minimisation, the cold truth is that all public bodies can save money by promoting the good old 'three R's: reduce, reuse, recycle'.

London Borough of Ealing

Approach
A local authority sought not only to deliver refuse and recycling services but also to achieve long-term waste minimisation. The local authority's vision matched with the strong track record of the social enterprise in delivering previous recycling services, and they now work together to effectively reduce waste while also developing local jobs, promoting social inclusion, and saving the local council money.

Service supplied
Full waste minimisation solution, including refuse and recyclables collection, recycling, and street cleansing.

Background
London Borough of Ealing's relationship with ECT Group goes back about 25 years, when the voluntary service council allocated grant money for the establishment of Ealing Community Transport to compensate for budget cuts in social services transport provision. The Council and ECT Group have both evolved, and ECT Group now encompasses not only Ealing Community Transport but also a range of waste minimisation services serving Ealing and other councils within and outside London.

The Council started contracting with ECT Group for recycling services in 1997, when it first awarded ECT Group a contract for kerbside recycling. At that time, recycling was a newer concept but rising on the political agenda. ECT Group had been delivering a similar contract in the neighbouring borough since 1996 so was well placed to deliver the contract.

The boroughwide contract with Ealing was implemented over a two-year period, going fully boroughwide in 1999. During this contract, ECT Group developed a new model for kitchen waste removal, the first of its kind in the UK. Andy Bond, managing director at ECT Group, explains, "After a trip to Milan, we noticed they were collecting kitchen waste there, so we secured some funding from London Remade to pilot a scheme, and it found its way into our major contracts; you just put your kitchen caddy out along with the kerbside recycling." The Council took notice of ECT Group's innovation, and when it came time to re-issue the tender in 2001, ECT Group won with flying colours. This time, the Council added garden waste to the list of ECT Group's responsibilities, which ECT Group was able to demonstrate the capacity to deliver.

During the first piloting scheme, ECT Group had pushed the boundaries of waste minimisation. In combination with its other contracts, ECT Group had developed a GIS system to link socio-economic status to recycling behaviour. "Recycling is not a universally used service," explains Andy, "Usage is fundamentally a product of socio-economic factors, so we determined that if we started measuring those factors then we could become more efficient, kind of like 'waste sociology'." This GIS system enabled ECT Group to deliver increasingly efficient service to its clients, including Ealing Council. ECT Group then used the same technique to model its kitchen waste service.

Action
In 2004, the Council decided to pull together all of its waste-related contracts into one large contract focused on waste minimisation.

Legality
It may seem more like a fairy tale, but in the case of this contract, ECT Group's tender was simply better than the others. Given the size of the contract, an advertised cap of £12 million, the Council advertised the tender in OJEU and received a number of proposals, primarily from the top international waste management businesses. Earl McKenzie, Head of Waste and Recycling at the Council, explains, "We set up the criteria to reflect quality and price at a ratio of 60:40 due to the flexibilities we sought in the contract."

From a financial perspective, ECT Group's proposal came in at £1 million *less* than the next lowest tender. From a quality perspective, Earl explains, "The other tenders had strengths but did not stretch or innovate to the extent required by Ealing at a time of root and branch organisational change. ECT best demonstrated understanding of the integrated nature of the contract, which is not the traditional set of separates but is led by recycling and waste; ECT understands waste minimisation, which is what 60 per cent of the contract is really about."

Not only was ECT Group's proposal cheaper and higher in quality, it was also clearer. "What's great about the ECT contract is that it's 100 per cent transparent; nothing hidden in there," adds Earl. "ECT put in relatively few caveats, which is where costs can really add up later because the price is only good if an exact set of conditions stay the same." Since the Council was seeking a flexible partner that would adapt over time, demonstrating the ability to alter services based on changing needs was crucial.

Economic impact

Straight off, the ECT Group contract was the cheapest proposal. There are other economic benefits though. Since ECT Group is a social enterprise and operates with social and environmental objectives while being a private business, it has a shared interest in seeing a reduction in waste and an improvement to the Ealing economy.

This is an important distinction because many waste management contracts contain perverse incentives. For instance, if the contract for recyclables is merely for the collection of them, then it becomes in the financial interest of the contractor to deliver that service as cheaply as possible. This can, in the worst scenarios, lead to the contractor actively discouraging people from recycling in the first place. As a result of ECT Group's work, the Council has saved money on landfill costs and gained savings in recycling credits.

As a social enterprise, ECT Group also seeks to work with people often labelled as 'hard-to-reach', which promotes local employment opportunities. ECT Group's depot operations in Ealing, funded through their contract with the Council and other councils, pays out over £1 million per year to employees living in the borough. Added to this figure are sundries like rent and local vehicle hire. While the Council's previous contract with ECT Group was about 60 per cent of the Ealing depot's total turnover, this income helps ECT Group leverage more resources, resulting in a respending of over £1.2 million in the local economy.

There is one added economic benefit that can be easily lost in situations like these: cross-subsidisation. ECT Group, again a social enterprise, actively re-invests its income into other parts of the business, primarily into its charitable parent company, Ealing Community Transport. ECT Group's re-investment into this charitable operation now outweighs the Council's own contribution. The Council is therefore cross-subsidising less profitable services merely by paying ECT Group to deliver competitive services (in other words, the Council is getting a community transport service without actually paying more for it!).

This point is crucial to public service delivery, because there is a tendency in the public sector to outsource (or privatise) public services. While it is true that the private sector may be able to deliver certain components of public services more efficiently, rarely can it deliver all aspects, especially pertaining to social exclusion. The result is a creaming off of the most profitable components of service delivery, leaving the public body with the financial burden of paying for the less profitable parts (or failing to deliver at all). In the case of this waste minimisation contract, the Council is not compromising quality at all to have this overall service delivered; however, it is worth the public sector considering the long-term economic impact of creaming off public services.

Additional impacts

"In comparison to other contractors the Council has worked with, we've found that the quality of staff training at ECT is better because there's more continuity and staff retention," Earl adds. "We don't get complaints from customers or lose customers and no other contractors come near to ECT as far as quality is concerned; I believe this is the opinion of the other local authorities as well." It's not always easy or possible to quantify achievements like staff retention or quality control, but the growing success of ECT Group testifies to the importance of these issues.

Earl also notes that ECT Group is solutions-oriented. In a typical private contract, any little change can result in a lengthy renegotiation of contract costs. Building on the success of ECT Group's open-book contract with a neighbouring council, the contract Ealing has just awarded is taking a similar approach. "We had quite a difficult time with our previous refuse contract," Earl explains. "It was an old-fashioned, adversarial relationship, full of defaults and clauses, which just led to an increase in price and created mistrust." The open-book system looks more like a partnership approach, with each organisation looking at how to best achieve the desired outcome, assessing financial implications and adjusting price *after* testing out new ideas.

The ability to be a partner is another reason ECT Group won the contract. "If we're going to get the best out of anything, then we have to have a genuine partnership because things change around a lot, such as weekly collection and recycling," notes Earl. "If we aren't able to manage the transition, then the costs could spiral out of control." The result can sometimes be savings. In ECT Group's other open-book contract, the organisation helped moved the borough's civic amenity (this is industry language for 'landfill') from a 5 to 50 per cent recycling rate for the same amount of money! This was achieved because the local councillor decided to make recycling mandatory. In an 'old-fashioned' relationship, the contractor would immediately raise the red flag about an increase in inputs and a need to raise the contract price. In this case, the partners waited out the results and found that ECT Group was able to manage the new volume using current resources (primarily because it had anticipated increased volume over time, so this was simply an expediting of that timeframe).

Next steps

The story of Ealing and ECT Group shows how a council can work with a local business to build it up and grow. ECT Group started off 25 years ago with an annual grant of about £400,000. Through a gradual expansion of services, to Ealing and to other councils, ECT Group has grown to be one of the largest social enterprises in the UK with a turnover of £24 million. With so much of that money going back into the local economy in the form of salaries and overheads, it is clearly in the interest of the Council to continue to promote the business's success.

Liverpool City Council

Approach

A council collaborated with a local social enterprise to find ways to deliver bulky waste removal more efficiently. The investment paid off by developing local jobs, promoting social inclusion, and saving the local council money.

Service supplied
Bulky waste removal and recycling.

Background
In 2000, Liverpool City Council had come to the end of its bulky waste removal and recycling contract with a mainstream contractor and was concerned about how it would continue to deliver the same or more extensive service under budgetary constraints. The Council's financial concern arose from the 'per collection' payment system it used with the previous contractor. "Under this system, we would pay say £10 per collection, which was fine under the rate of requests we had anticipated," explains David Hodnett, Environmental Manager for Regeneration at Liverpool City Council, "but we were getting more calls than we expected." The Council needed to find an economical way to promote a widespread service without going into debt.

At this time, politicians also wanted to work with the social enterprise sector to deliver public services. The Council began speaking with the FRC Group, based in Liverpool, which had a track record of providing socially minded business solutions for social and environmental issues.

Action
There had been political aspiration for the Council to work with social enterprises, but it still needed to address the financial bottom line. While FRC Group's training approach was effective, it understandably cost more than a mainstream approach that provided no training opportunities.

The Council solved this problem by splitting up funding for the bulky waste contract into two contracts: one contract explicitly for the delivery of bulky waste removal and recycling funded by the Council and one contract explicitly for the delivery of vocational training for hard-to-reach people, such as long-term unemployed people, funded by local Neighbourhood Renewal Fund money. This strategy enabled Bulky Bob's, the bulky waste subsidiary of FRC Group, to compete and win the contract because, unlike its mainstream competitors, it could combine mainstream service delivery and vocational training very efficiently since it had been delivering training for many years.

"Bulky Bob's also clearly understood its client base better than the competition," notes David. "Not only is their literature smooth and slick like everyone else's," he explains, "but when we had them explain their work to others, they offered a colourful and congenial presentation that was clearly in the spirit of partnership and co-operation. The traditional contractors usually turn up in their grey suits and just tell us 'this is how you will do this and this is what you will do'."

The Council's greater concern was how to continue providing a quality service under budgetary constraints. The payment structure the Council agreed with Bulky Bob's maintained payment per collection for the first two years of the contract with the expectation of paying Bulky Bob's an annual lump sum thereafter. By 2002, when the contract moved into lump sum payment, Bulky Bob's was receiving upwards of 50,000 calls per year (over 200 calls per day). The annual lump sum payment gave Bulky Bob's the needed leeway to invest in vans and infrastructure at a lower per-unit cost as well as to build personnel capacity.

Since this time, Bulky Bob's has met the 50,000 calls per year on the same budget as the Council was previously paying for 29,000 calls! In fact, as David mentions, "We've just been audited, and they did find that this new contract is working out cheaper than the previous one!"

Legality

Separating the basic service (bulky waste) from the social service (vocational training) made awarding the two contracts more clear-cut. Both were awarded to the financially competitive bidder. Some councils feel there will be concerns over quality versus price considerations, especially when combining social services elements, like employment training, with basic service contracts. The separation enabled Liverpool City Council to be very clear about what it was and was not paying for; it also levelled the playing field for social enterprises like Bulky Bob's, who could do both waste service and training quite effectively but could not compete against a mainstream business that was delivering the service exclusive of training.

The payment terms are also legal. David explains, "This contract was fundamentally different than the previous one because we used to pay for every collection they did, and now we pay a set figure for the year, and they agree to collect." Bulky Bob's had an advantage in this situation because the company measures success along social, environmental, and economic lines, not just economic. David concedes, "I'm not sure if this sort of thing was proposed before, but I don't think the old contractor would have done it." Whether or not your prospective contractor wants to agree to such a payment scheme, it is nevertheless legally acceptable.

Economic impact

First, Liverpool City Council has managed to provide a wider service for the same amount of money. That's no mean feat for any public body.

Second, the Council has reduced its landfill costs. Bulky Bob's is required to recycle at least 30 per cent of what they collect; they currently recycle 36 per cent. With a landfill tax credit of £18 per tonne, the Council has saved over £15,000 in the last year from the increased re-use and recycling of bulky waste alone.

Third, an LM3 evaluation of the Bulky Bob's contract with Liverpool City Council found a score of 2.65. That means that every £100 that the Council spends on bulky waste removal and recycling with Bulky Bob's generates an additional £165 for the local economy. This high impact arises from the fact that Bulky Bob's is based in Liverpool, employs local people, and uses local suppliers where possible.

Additional impacts

Liverpool City Council has identified a number of other benefits from the relationship with Bulky Bob's.

First, "There is a general feel-good factor that the public has," David explains, "knowing that their old items are going to help out less fortunate people and also about the fact that we are getting unemployed people into jobs." This knowledge fosters a more co-operative spirit, and David notes that, "people make the extra effort, which is why we've seen such high call rates."

Second, Bulky Bob's has delivered a better service. One major innovation has been the collection of items from inside the home. "Bulky Bob's recognised that there could be an old lady who has no way of getting her sofa out to the front of the house," David remarks, "so on their own initiative, they agreed to go inside the house and get stuff, obviously as long as the client signs a disclaimer about damages." David further explains, "Under a traditional contract arrangement, the response would be, 'we can only collect from the front' or 'if we have to go in it will cost more'. That's the difference."

Finally, the Council has been able to use Bulky Bob's for last minute work that would have otherwise cost a lot more to deliver. David mentions one instance, "where we had to deliver a lot of wheeled bins, and rather than go through a lengthy negotiating process with a traditional contractor, we were able to pay Bulky Bob's operatives overtime, and they knew the city well already." David also reflects on a recent neighbourhood clean-up campaign, "It was great because Bulky Bob's agreed to send a vehicle to this neighbourhood for the day, so residents were able to just get their bulky items removed at the same time as cleaning up their neighbourhood. It was also good publicity for Bulky Bob's so they sent a team along at no charge. We have also tried to reciprocate by letting them display their refurbished goods at a local market."

Next steps

The service provided by Bulky Bob's has been so exceptional that the Council is now discussing extending the contract. They're also discussing new ways of working. One major change under consideration is expanded hours. "It's a nine-to-five job at the moment," David explains, "so we're looking at adding evening or weekend collections since customers can't always be at home during business hours; we might need to make a nominal charge for this enhanced service, but it would help out a lot of people."

Youth services

> **Key points**
> - Developing a local solution to youth education succeeded in promoting the social inclusion of young people.
>
> - A local authority was able to foster a social enterprise to meet market gaps that saved the local authority money.
>
> - Promoting a local solution to youth education needs also promoted the local environment and local economy.
>
> - Promoting local enterprises to meet market gaps enabled these businesses to access new markets, bringing more income into the local economy.

The public sector cannot buy happy, productive children that grow into happy, productive adults in the same way that it can buy stationery. The public sector can, however, use its spending power to promote a healthy society as much as possible. No one doubts that investing in young people pays off later on. The hard part is allocating the budget for a pay-off that is a generation down the line. We won't know how the children in the case studies below will grow over the next two decades, but we do know that more creative solutions to youth services are not only socially but also economically prudent now.

Lincolnshire County Council

Approach
A local council found that one of the most successful ways to get socially excluded young people back on track was by pairing them with the leaders of a local community-managed woodland for unconventional education. The community got a quality natural resource, the young people found a way to constructively participate in society, and the Council saved money.

Service supplied
Youth development and education and woodland maintenance.

Background
In 2001, central government required Local Education Authorities (LEAs) to begin finding ways to provide full-time education for young people excluded from school. For Lincolnshire County Council, that meant finding ways to inspire 240 young people, some involved in anti-social behaviour, to commit themselves to giving learning another try. Sue Fenton-Smith, Head of Emotional and Behavioural Support Service at Lincolnshire County Council, worked with others at the Council to start a programme to address the young people's needs, called Solutions 4. "School is about education and accreditation," explains Sue, "whereas Solutions 4 is about citizenship and key messages about what is and isn't accepted in society."

With this broader goal of inspiring young people to feel a sense of citizenship, Sue needed to find different educational environments that would encourage rather than discourage their attendance. "We knew it was no good expecting these youngsters to go back into a setting that still had the parameters of normal school," notes Sue. "They'd kicked against that, and we needed to find something that was different." Finding something different offered the Council a chance to get creative. Driving through the county in search of different sites for schooling, Solutions 4 found a community woodland, Hill Holt Wood, and simply dropped in.

Hill Holt Wood (HHW) is a 14-hectare deciduous woodland situated on the Lincolnshire and Nottinghamshire border. Its owners bought the woodland in

1995 and have since developed a community-controlled social enterprise that employs 14 people. In an area where two-thirds of businesses employ less than five people, this makes HHW one of the largest businesses in the county. As one of 12 community woodlands in England, HHW aims to run and operate a self-sustaining woodland using traditional crafts incorporating modern techniques that benefit and are beneficial to the environment. To this day, HHW only receives 10 per cent of its turnover through grants that are exclusively for capital projects rather than service delivery. Before Solutions 4 approached HHW, the owners ran some educational workshops as part of the New Deal Environmental Task Force but nothing as formal as off-site schooling.

Action

The first step was to assess the interest and capacity of HHW to deliver a Solutions 4 scheme. Sue notes, "Hill Holt Wood was very interested in being able to put something back into the community, and they could see that it was also a way to share with youngsters their philosophy about looking after our world." HHW didn't have qualified experience working with young people, so the Council trained the on-site staff in behaviour management and other relevant issues.

There is no set curriculum for Solutions 4 schemes, so the Council and HHW co-developed a curriculum that was flexible and accountable to central government standards. HHW currently works with 24 students, offering a combination of education and vocational training, as some of the young people will go onto higher education while others will go into jobs.

The key issue is that HHW is an alternative setting to normal school. "Solutions 4 is about settings like Hill Holt Wood, insomuch that youngsters with pent up feelings enjoy being outside, can see immediate achievements in the work they're doing," explains Sue. "It's about opening their minds to what they could be successful with, and that's also where vocational achievement comes in, but you can't replicate what's happening in schools and you can't use teachers to do this work." In the instance of HHW and other off-site schemes, the teacher is a skilled craftsman, "and because they're skilled in something interesting to the youngsters," explains Sue, "they really get respect that way".

Finally, the Solutions 4 sites seek to create an open and supportive environment for participating young people. "They don't wear uniforms and there are smoking breaks, though we support them in kicking the habit," explains Sue. "They don't get excluded if they come on-site with drugs, and if they've been involved with the police due to violence or if they've got an anti-social disorder, we have to work through that with them." Such openness may shock many LEAs, but the success rates of Solutions 4 show that it works.

Legality

This case study outlines an approach for social service provision, since youth education is not strictly a procurement of goods or services. Solutions 4 has a budget and targets, and spending on off-site schemes is judged against performance. Selecting sites, however, is not subject to an OJEU process.

Economic impact

The Solutions 4 programme has been extraordinarily successful, and LEAs across the UK are seeking to replicate the model. Most of the impacts are difficult to measure, but HHW used LM3 to measure its economic impact to demonstrate how their collaboration on Solutions 4 is also important to maintaining a healthy local economy. HHW found that its LM3 as an organisation was 2.31. This means that every £100 entering HHW generates an additional £131 for the surrounding area. Considering that the Council has 24 children placed with HHW, that's a significant impact.

What's also important in this example is that the Council's collaboration with HHW for public service delivery enables HHW to operate a community woodland that serves additional functions yet doesn't require grant funding. In essence, HHW is able to cross-subsidise less profitable services, such as keeping the community woodland available and usable by the public, through its income from work with the Council. This is also possible because the work with the Council, which was enhanced by Solutions 4, has enabled HHW to access additional markets in youth services. HHW now collaborates with other councils on delivering alternative education, the Learning Skills Council's E2E programme, and the County Youth Service summer 'Uproject'. The Council therefore gets a community woodland for no additional cost to its budget.

Additional impacts

The first marker of the impact of Solutions 4 is its success rate. Sue notes, "We're only in the third year of the project so the youngsters haven't moved on yet, but already we've recorded excellent attendance rates." While quantifying a decrease in juvenile crime is difficult, police departments across the county have openly offered strong support for the programme because it seems to be contributing to a reduction in crime and anti-social behaviour:

> *"Lincolnshire Police has had a long and successful relationship with Nigel Lowthrop and Hill Holt Wood. We commend any initiative that engages with young people and diverts them away from anti-social or criminal activities. Hill Holt Wood has repeatedly demonstrated its ability to do this with individuals who have not responded to more recognised and conventional types of engagements. Furthermore, the young people from the Lincolnshire area who have experienced Hill Holt Wood have generally*

stayed out of the offending and anti-social cycle. They have gone on to contribute positively towards society with the skills they have obtained and become an asset, rather than a drain on their local communities."

Nigel Kay, Chief Inspector and Acting Community Safety Officer for the Lincolnshire Police Authority.

The strong language used by Nigel Kay reflects the degree to which youth education can impact on crime. Similarly, public bodies can promote social inclusion through the delivery of services that are not directly tied to social inclusion.

There is also an alternative cost to not developing local solutions for youth development. Many of the young people that HHW works with through Solutions 4 would otherwise be placed in provision outside the county. In addition to relocating the young person outside his/her home area, the provision can be extremely costly, averaging £70,000 per year. By providing a number of opportunities and locations for Solutions 4 within Lincolnshire, the LEA can save money and achieve better results.

Another impact that will be felt in several years is the development of a skilled workforce within the county. "Especially in Lincolnshire, where the skills are not always there," explains Sue, "we get a lot of youngsters coming from the south to do trade work." So all of the young people coming out of the Solutions 4 programme with accreditation will then become part of a skilled workforce in the community. "Now all we need to do is educate local businesses that NVQ3 is equivalent to GCSE in other subjects," explains Sue, "and they'll feel comfortable taking them into employment."[38]

There is an increasing body of research that empirically links health and economic development. All people benefit from having access to woodlands, which fosters regular exercise. Among young people, research has found a particularly useful role for outdoor activity in assisting children with Attention Deficit Disorder. Specific to HHW, many of the young people coming from difficult home lives have demonstrated markedly calmer behaviour after participating in training and development schemes at HHW.

Finally, the focus of Solutions 4 is to equip young people with the skills and confidence to go onto higher education or employment. Crime research has found that securing a decent job is the most significant factor in decreasing re-offending rates.[39] This has a clear economic value to the public sector.

---

[38] NVQ3 stands for National Vocational Qualification Level 3 and more information is available at www.dfes.gov.uk/nvq. GCSE stands for General Certificate of Secondary Education and more information is available at www.dfes.gov.uk/qualifications

[39] There are a number of studies on this, including *Reducing re-offending by ex-prisoners*, Social Exclusion Unit, July 2002.

Next steps

This approach to youth development has been so successful that other areas are looking at replicating the model. Lincolnshire County Council is currently reviewing the accreditation pathway for Solutions 4 in light of the Department for Education and Skills' *14–19 Education and Skills* White Paper.[40]

Gloucestershire County Council

Approach

A county council developed a competitive local alternative to placing children in out-of-area foster care organisations. The local alternative now provides specialised services that meet the needs of local children, and the Council has historically spent less money on placements than on out-of-area alternatives.

Service supplied

Foster care placement and management by Community Foster Care

Background

Like many councils, Gloucestershire County Council employs in-house foster carers. On occasion, however, the needs of the child exceed the capacity of the in-house carers, so the Council must place the child with an external agency. Patricia Lomax, Purchasing Officer for Children's Services, explains, "We're part of the South West Purchasing Group (SWPG), which is comprised of 15 local authorities, and we have a database of about 900 providers for different types of care." The Council currently uses about 11 agencies in the UK to deliver foster care services.

Action

In 1997, before the SWPG had formed its database, the Council determined that there was a market gap for local carers. "It made a lot of sense," Patricia explains. "We wanted to set up an organisation that would employ local people to meet local children's needs and contribute to the local economy." The Council, via the Social Services budget, invested £70,000 to set up a local foster care organisation, called Community Foster Care (CFC). The Council began placing children with CFC soon thereafter and currently has 13 children placed there.

There are two components to CFC that have maintained its market niche since 1997. First, "Our current placement pattern with CFC is for children who have been with them for a number of years and for whom CFC have been able to provide

---

40 Department for Education and Skills (2005) *14–19 Education and Skills* (London: HMSO).

permanence", Patricia explains. "They're known as 'permanent placements' because they will most likely be there through to adulthood." Second, CFC has always been able to guarantee Gloucestershire County Council competitive rates.

Legality

Foster care is a service provision rather than a strict procurement of goods and services, so councils can look at a wide range of factors in selecting carers. Councils are nevertheless constrained by their budgets, so they do have to be prudent in making these decisions. The Council reviews which care organisations are both best matched to the child's needs and also have a vacancy. While the Council does not use CFC as a preferred provider, CFC's rates are competitive with or often cheaper than the competition, which makes it a viable option when a child's needs profile matches CFC's profile.

Economic impact

The Council invested £70,000 eight years ago to start up CFC. Was it worth it? Patricia notes, "Obviously, our motivation was the welfare of the children, but yes, from a financial perspective we have saved money from this strategy." And not a small amount either. Paying a more competitive rate for the 13 children currently placed with CFC, who can charge up to 75 per cent less than other agencies, Gloucestershire County Council is saving tens of thousands of pounds each year.

A breakdown of Gloucestershire County Council's contract with CFC found that CFC re-invested three-quarters of its contract back into the local economy. This high percentage is due to the fact that all of CFC's carers come from the local area (the county in this instance), and CFC pays rent, professional fees, and overheads like printing and photocopying to local businesses.

Additional impacts

CFC has been recognised as a leader in foster care for several years. The Chief Executive won the *New Statesman*'s Young Social Entrepreneur of the Year in 2003, and CFC was a finalist in the Social Enterprise Coalition's Social Enterprise of the Year in 2004. CFC's social enterprise mission means that the company provides its service not only effectively but also by working constructively with the community it serves.

As Patricia is keen to point out, "One of the most important implications of this work is that the children stay in Gloucestershire."

Next steps

The Council continues to use CFC for placements, although there is now an emphasis to employ more in-house carers.

Back office services

Key points
- A creative approach to a private car hire contract gave all public bodies in the region a more competitive solution.

- Using a social enterprise enabled a local authority to deliver cleaning services while also promoting social inclusion.

- Public bodies used their spending on 'back office' services to achieve regeneration targets that other public bodies seek to achieve through spending via 'frontline' services.

- Every way that the public sector spends money has the potential to achieve regeneration aims.

We tend to divide up public spending between that which is explicitly dedicated for public services, such as domiciliary care or homeless services, and that which we consider to be mundane expenditures, such as stationery and premises cleaning.

Many of the case studies in this publication demonstrate how public bodies are achieving regeneration through delivering a range of services. Quite a few public bodies would consider school food to be a background expenditure compared to, say, books; however, the work at St Peter's showed that school meals become just as much a part of a student's education as learning to read. In government parlance, activities that are not considered core to the actual public service are called 'back office'. Meanwhile, the actual service, the one with which the public actively interfaces, is called the 'frontline service'.

University of Wales Institute Cardiff (UWIC)/ Welsh Procurement Initiative

Approach
A Welsh university, in conjunction with the National Assembly for Wales's Welsh Procurement Initiative, used the renewal of a car hire framework contract to pilot the strategy for an all-Wales service contract divided into regional components that would deliver locally focused service with regional economic benefits at nationally competitive prices.

Service supplied
Self-drive vehicle hire (car hire).

Background
Set up in 2002, the Welsh Procurement Initiative (WPI) aims to improve the efficacy of the Welsh public sector, for example through collaboration and sharing best practice, seeking to develop SMEs, and advancing the sustainability agenda. The WPI, through consultation with Welsh public sector organisations, flagged up car hire contracts as an opportunity to pilot the concept of cross-sector collaboration for two reasons. Peter Standfast, Head of Procurement at University of Wales Institute Cardiff (UWIC), explains, "The current provision was not ideal and the service was not considered 'sector-specific'." In other words, the public bodies involved knew they could do better, and car hire needs were similar enough across the public bodies involved to join up on one contract.

Most organisations have requirements for the provision of self-drive vehicles, which is the more formal term for car hire. As Peter explains, "Organisations that have a regular and consistent requirement often lease or contract for pool cars; organisations with a less consistent requirement or with multiple sites, where the efficient management of a pool fleet is much more complex, generally set up 'spot hire' arrangements." Spot hire arrangements simply mean that the price paid for vehicles is agreed, but the requirements are dictated by ad hoc demand.

A benchmarking exercise led by UWIC of both collaborative and local car hire arrangements in Wales found a large variation in hire tariffs and service levels. The spread between the lowest and highest daily hire tariffs for commonly used saloon cars, even for long-standing contracts, ranged from £23 to £40. The desire to achieve a fair price for all contracting organisations that reflected a competitive price in all locations prompted the WPI to attempt to develop a car hire tender covering all public bodies in Wales.

Although a UK-wide car hire contract existed in the higher education sector, organised by the National Vehicle Hire Discussion Group, UWIC and the University of Glamorgan had previously opted out of it. "We found that the national arrangements did not best serve our needs," explains Peter. "The UK-wide pricing might have been beneficial for other areas, but we were able to get a much better price in southeast Wales than the Discussion Group." Since the current car hire contract was coming up for retendering in 2002, shortly after the WPI had identified car hire as a market opportunity, UWIC and University of Glamorgan volunteered to lead the tendering process for a contract available to all Welsh public bodies. UWIC undertook the role of contracting organisation.

Action

"Since UWIC had opted out of the UK-wide contracts in the past because it did not meet our specific needs," explains Peter, "we were keen to ensure that the Wales-wide contract could meet the needs of a very diverse set of public bodies." All Welsh public bodies were invited to indicate their potential support and utilisation of a Wales-wide car hire contract, and UWIC received a favourable response from 29 public bodies (representing a 25 per cent response rate). UWIC organised a project board with a number of the public bodies that had indicated interest in the tender to ensure that tender documentation met the requirements of everyone taking part.

The planning board decided to split the framework agreement into five regional components to ensure not only that regional variations in demand and expectations could be met but also that providers were given a realistic opportunity to win business. Since the overall contract value was worth an estimated £3 million pounds over three years, Peter knew UWIC would need to follow the OJEU process.

The planning board recognised that while all the national and international car hire providers were very familiar with the OJEU process, many SMEs in the UK were still either completely unaware of the OJEU or unsure how to best search for opportunities. "Since one of the goals of the WPI is to foster more competitive Welsh businesses," explains Peter, "we tried to establish the identities of local car hire providers who might not be aware of the OJEU requirements." Peter wanted to ensure that as many organisations as possible had opportunities to bid for elements of the business. In addition to simply asking the participating organisations to identify potential firms in their geographic areas, UWIC also searched the Internet and published directories. Peter then rang the firms identified, informed them of the background and potential of this contract, and invited them to submit an expression of interest to participate in the tendering process.

UWIC received an expression of interest from 17 firms, ranging from international chains to locally based small independent companies. UWIC then invited the 17 firms to return a pre-qualification questionnaire, which all but one firm returned.

An evaluation panel developed a scoring system to measure and rank the legal and financial status of those wishing to bid and to establish their ability to meet the participants' requirements. At this stage the panel was content with the status and suitability of all firms that had returned the pre-qualification document and formally invited all firms to tender.

The tender documents were issued with bidders given just over six weeks to respond. A total of ten companies submitted tenders, seven of which would be considered UK national or multinational organisations and three organisations based in Wales.

After evaluating aspects such as pricing, geographic coverage, size of available fleet, commitments to good service levels, and existing client references, the evaluation panel selected recipients to cover all of Wales. The panel selected the two highest scoring suppliers for South Wales and North Wales and one supplier covering Mid-Wales, as well as a supplier providing a 'back-up service' for the entirety of Wales. "We then invited these suppliers for interview and pre-contract discussions," explains Peter, "and it was here that we were able to focus the dialogue on specific potential clients, areas of service, and relevant operational detail."

Legality

UWIC followed all the EU rules on advertising, evaluating, and awarding contracts. The part that many public bodies shy away from is proactively seeking out local businesses. As in other case studies, there is nothing wrong with seeking out businesses and advising them of opportunities to bid for a contract once that contract is made public. And as it turned out for the UWIC car hire contract, getting more businesses to tender boosted the competition for the contract, ultimately securing the best combination of service providers for the Welsh public sector.

Economic impact

"Gauging the precise economic impact of a contract like this is tough," explains Peter. "There is no formal commitment to quantity, organisations may commence participating at any time during the contract term, and in this case it is the first contract of its kind for Wales."

There is nevertheless considerable scope for promoting local economic development through the contract. The overall contract itself is anticipated to be worth £2-3 million per year, depending upon how many organisations ultimately end up participating. "Spending with the five nominated suppliers will certainly be in excess of £1 million in the first full year of the contract," explains Peter, "and at least half of that is with the Welsh-based companies." Peter continues, "Even spending with the national providers has a local economic impact though, as to service the accounts effectively, these suppliers must have local depots employing local staff." This might constitute a further opportunity to develop local businesses.

Above all, the public bodies involved are achieving a competitive price by diversifying the supply base to include a range of businesses sizes. "The growing support for these contracts within the Welsh public sector is based very much on the improved pricing obtained," explains Peter, "coupled with the good service levels and 'local' availability offered by the various suppliers."

Additional impacts

In addition to obtaining better pricing through the aggregation of the expenditure, the division into regional components has meant that all public sector organisations in Wales have access to car hire arrangements that are locally provided with consistent levels of service.

UWIC and WPI, together with members of the project board, also monitor and manage the contract through reviews of management information and customer feedback together with periodic review meetings with the various suppliers.

Next steps

"One of the benefits derived from this exercise has been the proving of the benefit of dividing contract opportunities into regional components," explains Peter, "and the WPI is adopting this approach as an effective way of optimising expenditure without restricting competition, and many of the future collaborative contracts in the Welsh public sector will follow this 'regional components' model." As a framework agreement, breaking down the contract into regional components is justifiable since it served to diversify the supply base, promote competition, and achieve a lower cost overall.

Reading Borough Council

Reading Borough Council has been contracting with Greenboro Ltd since 1990 for the provision of premises cleaning. Cleaning of premises is not a glamorous subject in public spending discussions. It's also an inward-facing service, meaning that it is for the benefit of the Council and not a public service in the way we think of domiciliary care or homeless services. Nevertheless, Reading Borough Council has managed to turn a mundane behind-the-scenes service (often termed 'back office') into a vehicle for social inclusion.

Greenboro is a social firm, which means that it seeks to bring people often labelled as 'hard-to-reach' into the labour market, particularly those with learning disabilities. It operates as a private business but, as a social firm, re-invests its profits back into the organisation. Working with such an organisation is also in the interest of the Council because it enables it to achieve government-issued targets on social inclusion. Under the 2001 Department of Health's *Valuing People* White Paper, "Government will provide new opportunities for children and adults with learning disabilities and their families to live full and independent lives as part of their local communities."[41] There are now set targets related to this issue.

---

41 Department of Health (2001) *Valuing People: A New Strategy for Learning Disability for the 21st Century* (HMSO).

By working with Greenboro, Reading Borough Council has not only secured a competitive service but also made strides to achieving social inclusion of people with learning disabilities. The other added benefit for the Council is that it promotes local regeneration by working with a locally based business that then re-invests its spending on suppliers and staff, many of whom come from disadvantaged communities in the area.

The fact that neither organisation can precisely remember how work started 15 years ago highlights an important point when it comes to changing mindsets: the integration of social inclusion goals into basic procurement needs can be a mainstream idea! No one raises flags now about Greenboro being a social firm; it is simply the current service provider that consistently provides a quality service at a competitive rate.

University of Vermont, USA: The impact of higher education[42]

Universities and other large education institutions are frequently the largest employers in an area; they are also an important employer as they are likely to endure any economic fluctuations. Universities in the USA approach town–gown relations and local economic development more substantially than in the UK. Most of the major universities, such as the more famous Harvard and Yale Universities, operate entire offices with full-time employees dedicated to community relations, including local economic development. The investment arises from the intense competition among universities, where location becomes a major selling point. Many universities, particularly publicly funded ones, are required in their charters to benefit their home states.

The University of Vermont (UVM), the state university for Vermont, evaluated its economic impacts across the board in order to develop employment and purchasing policies to help strengthen the local economy while still meeting the University's needs. Conducted by the UVM/Burlington Community Outreach Partnership Center, the aim of the project is to increase the opportunities for employment and advancement of low-income residents living in Burlington's Old North End and adjoining neighbourhoods. In addition to generating direct employment, UVM believes that if it can better link University purchasing to local and Vermont businesses, this increased economic activity will stimulate business development and indirect employment opportunities for residents.

---

42 Much of this case study is documented in UVM (2001) *The Impact of UVM's Employment and Purchasing Practices On Local Business and Low Income Residents: Update* (Vermont: University of Vermont).

Evaluation methodology

The project team surveyed residents of the most disadvantaged neighbourhood in the area, known as the Old North End (ONE), to understand local capacity and needs. The team discovered that over two-thirds of UVM staff who lived in the ONE are employed in pay ranges that fall below the liveable wage for single parents, which a large proportion of the ONE residents are. About 73 per cent of residents do not have education beyond high school level (equivalent to UK sixth form), which is usually a requirement for the higher-paid jobs at UVM.

While this picture might come across as dire, the UVM team found that the workforce was reasonably skilled and motivated. Nearly half of those surveyed possessed an average of six years of experience in relevant fields and all those surveyed who were unemployed were actively seeking employment.

UVM also evaluated purchasing data for the University, categorising about $106 million worth of expenditures by industrial sector and by whether the funds went to local or out-of-state vendors. The team then plugged these figures into an economic modelling system known as RIMS II (Regional Industrial Multiplier System) to find out what the potential multiplier effect of that spending would be in the region. The system is based on data collected periodically and aggregated by sector. UVM also divided up the University's spending into sector, using the 'standard industrial code' system, which is compatible with RIMS II.

While a lot of detail is lost about individual suppliers, the process enabled UVM to see the bigger picture. The project team found that about half of UVM's expenditures went out-of-state and almost 75 per cent of UVM's spending fell within four major sectors: services, trade contracting, manufacturing, and retail. UVM also discovered that some industrial sectors have a high RIMS II local multiplier effect, yet the University currently purchases little from in-state businesses in these sectors. This, for instance, marks an opportunity for UVM to change some of its spending to benefit Vermont.

Issues identified

In response to the lack of local knowledge about UVM employment opportunities and application procedures, UVM's employment office began bi-monthly information sessions in the ONE to address questions about UVM employment. The University also provided assistance with CVs and the application process.

To increase local purchasing, UVM created and disseminated a brochure to local businesses on how to do business with UVM. At the policy level the project team determined that a local purchasing policy directed at those sectors with high local multipliers and some existing local vendors would not only support local businesses but also increase the local capacity to provide those goods and services over time. The larger and more diverse supply base would reduce market prices, thereby reducing the prices UVM must pay for goods and services. So from an entirely selfish perspective, contributing to local economic development is a contribution to UVM.

The team realistically identified that local purchasing cannot universally provide lower prices and greater selection, and they did not recommend a universal policy that UVM buy locally. The project team used the RIMS II analysis to identify which sectors would provide the best opportunity for future local sourcing. Since the RIMS II analysis showed certain areas where local sourcing might be more beneficial, the project team determined that the University develop a targeted local purchasing policy that favours vendors in certain sectors.

The project team also remarked on the value of non-locally based businesses to the local economy. Three of UVM's largest contracts are with Staples (office suppliers), Fisher (scientific and medical supplies), and Sodexho Marriott (food services). These three companies maintain headquarters and distribution hubs outside of Vermont, but they are strong contributors to the local economy. The project team found, for instance, that Sodexho Marriott is similar in some ways to an in-state firm: It employs hundreds of local residents, pays comparable salaries as those to UVM employees, purchases food from over a dozen Vermont food vendors, and some dining facilities purchase up to 50 per cent of their food from local businesses. Profits of these firms, however, often do not stay within the state.

The project team also noted that institutions are often linked to the businesses they use, and bad behaviour by the larger companies might reflect poorly on the University. The project team raised a case from the 1980s, when many institutions were criticised and boycotted for their investments in South Africa's then-apartheid government. UVM could diminish its public image if it were to find itself in a partnership with a socially unappealing company.

Recommendations

The project team's primary goal was to promote local employment opportunities. In addition to direct collaboration with the community, it also identified ways that UVM could indirectly contribute to local employment opportunities through its purchasing behaviour:

- Increase information on UVM produce and service needs to current and potential vendors.

- Secure additional information about local vendors.

- Provide more information within UVM about local vendors to increase opportunities for local vendors to sell to the University.

The project team's recommendations demonstrate a crucial link: promoting local employment opportunities is not just linked to education and training but also to the University's own purchasing behaviour.

Action taken

The recommendations led to the formation of two working groups, one on employment and one on purchasing.

The employment group has since:

- Set up monthly meetings with an employment centre to discuss employment opportunities with UVM.

- Instituted training, mentoring, and placement programmes for work across UVM for individuals with learning disabilities or moving off of public assistance.

- Worked with students to develop a brochure to encourage more UVM departments and individuals to act as 'professional peers' to local residents facing barriers to employment.

- Worked with students to develop a 'broadcast fax' system for the UVM employment office to send out job notices to workforce development and placement organisations.

Meanwhile, the purchasing group has since:

- Put UVM's contract opportunities on the Vermont state tendering website.

- Worked with students to contact businesses in the ONE to promote their use of 'Catscratch', the student charge card system.

- Created a website for UVM departments and other de-centralised UVM purchasers that provides information on local businesses and discount programmes available to UVM.

- Developed a section on why, how, and when to increase purchasing from Vermont business for a wider staff-training module on finance and accounting.

Next steps

The project team issued a report, *The Impact of UVM's Employment and Purchasing Policies and Practices on Local Businesses and Lower Income Residents*, in 2001. Since then, the University has continued its efforts to increase employment from local disadvantaged groups and to inform local businesses of supplier opportunities at UVM. Adoption of a targeted local purchasing policy is on hold with the arrival of a new administration at the University.

Resources

The policy documents referred to in this publication that back up the case for more creative approaches to public procurement include:

National Strategy for Neighbourhood Renewal
Social Exclusion Unit, 2000
Website: www.neighbourhood.gov.uk

National Procurement Strategy for Local Government
ODPM, 2003
Website: www.odpm.gov.uk

Securing the future: The UK Sustainable Development Strategy
HM Treasury, 2005
Website: www.sustainable-development.gov.uk

Making the case for sustainable procurement: the NHS as a good corporate citizen
Health Development Agency (now National Institute for Health and Clinical Excellence), 2005
Website: www.hda-online.org.uk

If you are seeking more specific information on how you can promote social inclusion through public spending, see the following:

Proactive Procurement
Co-operatives UK, 2004
Website: www.co-opunion.coop

More for your money – a guide to social enterprise
Social Enterprise Coalition, 2005
Website: www.socialenterprise.org.uk

If you want more detailed information on tools that you can use to measure and improve the impact of public spending, see the following from nef:

Plugging the Leaks: making the most of every pound the enters your community

The Money Trail: measuring your impact on the local economy using LM3

Proving and Improving: a quality and impact toolkit for social enterprise

If you would like to follow up on the case studies, please contact the organisations cited directly or contact nef for more details.

Acknowledgements

This publication represents a collaborative effort to consolidate knowledge that seeks to catalyse change.

nef would like to thank the Commission for Rural Communities (an operating division of the Countryside Agency) for their long-term support of this work. We would also like to thank the European Social Fund Equal Programme (through the Social Enterprise Partnership (GB) Limited) for their support.

The Author would like to offer sincere gratitude to the many enterprises, organisations, and individuals who lent their time and energy to producing this publication:

David Atkinson, Commission for Rural Communities
Pegs Bailey, Forth Sector
James Belton, Forth Sector
Cheryle Berry, Lincolnshire County Council
Kevin Bishop, Welsh Local Government Association
Andy Bond, ECT Group
Amanda Brassington, Sheffield Rebuild
Beth Brewis, Forth Sector
Mike Brogan, Fusion 21
Nancy Brooks, University of Vermont (USA)
David Boyle, **nef**
Mark Burnett, Riverside Housing Association
Gord Cunningham, Coady Institute (Canada)
Amanda Daniel, Soil Association
Sue Fenton-Smith, Lincolnshire County Council
David Ford, Groundwork EBS
Sipi Hämeenaho, Mutual Advantage
Nathan Harrow, Cornwall Food Programme
Roy Heath, Cornwall Food Programme
Frances Hill, Ways and Means Trust
David Hodnett, Liverpool City Council
Jeanette Hughes, Forth Sector
Jennifer Inglis, Social Enterprise East Midlands

Tim Jackson, Sustainable Development Commission
Naomi Johnson, Community Recycling Network
Alan Kay, Community Business Scotland Network
Olivia Klevan, Social Enterprise Coalition
Paul Lewis, Social Enterprise Unit
Kirstin Liddell, Local Government Association
Deborah Littman, UNISON
Amy Longrigg, **nef**
Nigel Lowthrop, Hill Holt Wood
Patricia Lomax, Gloucestershire County Council
Kate MacDonald, Forth Sector
Darian McBain, NHS Purchasing and Supply Agency
Shonagh McEwan, Green Group in the Scottish Parliament
Stuart Mead, Commission for Rural Communities
Ken Meter, Crossroads Resource Center (USA)
Barry Mitchell, Northumberland County Council
Stacy Mitchell, Institute for Local Self-Reliance (USA)
John Montague, Newlife Regeneration Construction
Mary Murphy, **nef**
Gordon Murray, Improvement & Development Agency
Jeanette Orrey, St Peter's Church of England Primary School
Ruth Potts, **nef**
Heather Rankin, FRC Group
Alan Ratcliffe, Northumberland County Council
Katharine Rayner, Common Cause Co-operative
Andreas Reichstein, Erlacher Höhe (Germany)
Sally Reynolds, Social Firms UK
Tony Rich, Local Government Association
Kevin Robbie, Forth Sector
Richard Schramm, University of Vermont (USA)
Gerold Schwarz, Social Enterprise Partnership
Susannah Senior, Sustainable Development Commission
Janet Sharpe, Sheffield Homes
Bob Soames, Contracts Consultancy
Alan Smith, Office of the Deputy Prime Minister
Peter Smith, Procurement Excellence
Alison Standfast, Welsh Procurement Initiative
Peter Standfast, University of Wales Institute Cardiff
Bill Taylor, Riverside Housing Association
Jenny Thatcher, University of Bradford
Jean Tucker, Community Foster Care
Mark Turner, Groundwork EBS
Michelle van Toop, Yorkshire & Humber Centre of Excellence

Perry Walker, **nef**
Gareth Wall, Centre for Public Scrutiny
Matthew Walsham, Social Enterprise Coalition
Bernie Ward, **nef**
Jonathan Watson, Health Cluster Net
Adam Wilkinson, Northumberland County Council
Annette Williams, Devon County Council
Gordon Wordsworth, Sheffield Rebuild